SAVE AFRICA

A MODERN AFRICAN POETRY
ANTHOLOGY AND SHORT
STORIES

SAVE AFRICA

A MODERN AFRICAN POETRY
ANTHOLOGY AND SHORT
STORIES

DAVID GRETCH

Save Africa: A Modern African Poetry Anthology and Short Stories by David Gretch

This book is written to provide information and motivation to readers. Its purpose is not to render any type of psychological, legal, or professional advice of any kind. The content is the sole opinion and expression of the author, and not necessarily that of the publisher.

Copyright © 2021 by David Gretch

All rights reserved. No part of this book may be reproduced, transmitted, or distributed in any form by any means, including, but not limited to, recording, photocopying, or taking screenshots of parts of the book, without prior written permission from the author or the publisher. Brief quotations for noncommercial purposes, such as book reviews, permitted by Fair Use of the U.S. Copyright Law, are allowed without written permissions, as long as such quotations do not cause damage to the book's commercial value. For permissions, write to the publisher, whose address is stated below.

Printed in the United States of America.

ISBN 978-1-955363-00-6 (Paperback)
ISBN 978-1-955363-01-3 (Digital)

Lettra Press books may be ordered through booksellers or by contacting:

Lettra Press LLC
30 N Gould St. Suite 4753
Sheridan, WY 828011
1 307-200-3414 | info@lettrapress.com
www.lettrapress.com

CONTENTS

Foreword..xi
Natural Gift by Ngozi Olivia Osuoha… 1
Essay: Who Un-Africanized Us? by Nancy Ndeke…..................2

Poetry from South Africa
Morgana DientoLameculos
Cry, My Beloved Country… 9
Cold and Lifeless… 10

Poetry from Uganda
Kabedoopong Piddo Ddibe'st
Serve the Poet…...15
Ruping and Anyadwee…...18
Ruping and Anyadwee…...28
(The Ugly Ones Are Already Born)…...28
Ruping and Anyadwee…...34
(Love Confession)…...34
Ruping and Anyadwee…...38
(My Husband Sleeps with His Back Turned to Me).................38
A Voice in the Dark…...45
The Pearl 48
Ballad of the Five Foolish Virgins..50
Chess Game 55
The Virgin Raven 57
Song to the Guest…..58

Animal Meeting..59
Some Rise, Some Fall...76
Horns of the Unicorns..77
The Knotted Heart..84
Mammon..85
Weaverbirds..86
The Hair of the Monster...88
The Uninvited Guest...93
Upper Room 96
Mortal Dance...99
Ode to a Fallen Soldier... 101
One Bride, Two Husbands 105
The Promised Rape 109
Cosmetology 111

Obella Stephen
Queen of the Anthill.. 116
Raise No Weapons 118
The Weeping Africa.. 119
Death Certificate... 121
Bony Masses, Fat Leaders...123
Smoke from the Gunfire...124
Down the Streets...125
The Rat Ate the Cat 127
Blood and Quill 129
When I Am Gone 131

Edakasi Daniel
Grains of Peace..134
The Glory of a Pen 135
Don't Break My Ring... 137
Corruption 138
Unchain My Hands 139
The Blood of My Land 141

Poetry from Kenya
Nancy Ndeke
Africa 145
Bleeding Land 148
Blessed Curse 150
Bones 152
Dance 155
Devil's Price 157
Living 162
Memories 166
O Moses! 168
Potters 170
Poverty 172
Raise Hope 174
Some Facts 176
Stain 178
The Other Child 180
Untitled (This Bleeding Baby) 183
The Poet's Pot 185
Weeping Willows 187
Imported Answers 189
Thomas 191
Nancy 193
Sweet Divide 195
Freight 197

Benjamin Chelangat
Buried without Graves 200

Philip Mainge
Dying Africa 203
Disfranchised Woeful Africa 207

Dr. Joan Ngunnzi
I Have Heard 210
Duped 211
The Last Bullet 212
Stuck in Kismayu 213
Fire Foxes 214
Picture on the Wall 215
In This Life 216

Poetry from Nigeria
Ngozi Olivia Osuoha
Herdsmanization 221
Religious Beasts 223
Political Monsters 225
Campaign Promises, a Bunch of Balderdash 227
The Magic 230
Letter to Mandela 231
Bloodland 233
If We All Were Cattle 235
Punctured Nature 237
Poor God 240
Crusaders of Evil 242
Ages of War 243

Etim Bassey Onyan
The Untrodden Paths of Africa 247
Africa, Speak! 249

Nseobong Edem
The Hard Way 252
How, Brother? 254
Barbarian 256
We're All Guilty 258
Farewell Song 260

Save Africa from That Man 263
Sick Sinking Ship 265
Here's Not My Home 267
Brother's Blade 268

Chidi Nwosu
One Day 272
Gathering Storms 274
To Talk Is to Die 275

Francis Annagu
Our Land in a Desert Trough 277
Africa (A Child) 279
Song of Busi Mhlongo 280
Elephant 282

Udekwe Chikadibia
Tragic 284
I Was Made to Believe 285

Nosar Philips
Untitled (Eniyan) 287
Untitled (Amope) 289

David Chukwudi Njoku
Save Africa: The Preacher Bleeds 291
We Are Not Prisoners 294
Away with the Dead 296

Nwankwo Christian
I Am a Black, an African American 299

Ayomide Samuel
Magnificent Image 301

Valor Not by War..303

Abdulazeez Ishaq
The Oil Lamp 306
Riches after Ruins 308

Naphtali Festus Adda
Dear Plateau.. 311

Dan Okafor
Africa, Save Me!...313
The Effigy of Self-Righteousness.....................................317
The Oracle of Silence..322
Virtues of the Queen..325

Appendix
Book Review of Save Africa 329

FOREWORD

Francis Annagu uses poetry to denounce social inequalities, speak for the hoi poloi, yet praise the profound beauty of the people and culture of Africa. His poetry reflects many contemporary shifts that are somehow material aspects of the human condition and experiences, codified in an allegorical and metaphorical language. The poet sees himself as part of the narrative in his poems and as such is not excluded in the lively contexts in which the themes are woven. As language is vital to poetry, so are its topics and the portrait of social events and phenomena in his poems.

Benjamin Chelangat is a poet who is alive to the fact that Africa has to a great extent ceased to develop because of the greed for power, corruption, nepotism, tribalism and Civil Wars. He believes that by using his poetic pen as a weapon, he will be in a position to shoot down some excesses that have for years reduced Africa to being an object of ridicule. His poem "Buried without Graves" was inspired by his urge to unravel the consequences of wars not only in Africa but also across the whole world.

NATURAL GIFT
by Ngozi Olivia Osuoha

Rocky valley with green leaves,
Rushing water of real nature
As white as snow,
So rich to flow.

Rocky valley of waters,
Rocky waters of nature,
Site of health,
Site of healing.

Rocky valley of nature,
So divine a gift,
So great a lift.
Green, white, swift, a rift.

Rocky land of God
Flowing with milk and honey,
So lovely to behold,
So dear to be grateful for.

Rocky waters, rocky nature.
The waterfall for humankind.
Falling water for humanity,
Quenching thirst of scary quest.

ESSAY: WHO UN-AFRICANIZED US?

by Nancy Ndeke

Every culture has its plusses and a little less. All peoples have much to celebrate about their uniqueness because we are all children of our environment. We take from nature what our needs are and leave the rest for tomorrow stored in our DNA, passed onto our children. Some attributes we applaud, some we denounce, coming up with motley of measures to curb abuse and excess. Such is society in a nutshell.

Then there is Africa.

Noted for its generosity of spirit and warmth of its people, it is a land that is indeed beautiful to behold. However, this beauty, generosity, and warmth has been visited with horrid repercussions time and again with the passage of time since the first visitors landed on Africa's shores hunting for spices, slaves, elephant tusks, and the pure bliss of exotic sightings of a race of black men.

Africa welcomed the brave thugs and sold its children abroad to be treated as less than human on plantations thousands of miles away. Whether the seller understood the import of his action or not is not the current debate. The fact that it happened and continues to this day is the issue. The consequence is evident in the struggles for identity and in the bitterness of those uprooted from their motherlands, given new names and tongues up to this day. I need cite no examples. Freedom has been the song of these descendants of Mother Africa to date. Is this who the African is then, one who sells his own to an unknown for immediate gain?

There was not just the willing seller and the willing buyer in the enslaving of so many. There was also the raiding of whole communities by slave hunters encouraged by the buyers. It was a complex arrangement where trusts were abused in pursuit of profit and involved the abuse of another. Where then did the blame lie hundreds of years ago? Where is the blame now as more horror and evil is visited on Africa in the modern-day slave trade (read: human trafficking)?

Back to the African. He, the African, had no fence to keep his neighbor off his property. He celebrated his son and the son of his neighbor. He fed any stranger who came in peace. He gave a stranger land to settle and courted a wife for him. Evidence of this great generosity can be seen at all entry points in Africa by the seeds of foreigners who forever changed the local landscapes through intermarriages with the locals. So who de-Africanized the African, turning him from a warm and generous soul to a hard-nosed criminal selling the souls of his people to the highest bidder?

Is it the creeds that came with the visitors? Is it the monetarized commerce that replaced barter and trade, or is it the lifestyle of the visitor that rubbed off on the African?

For a man with a scholarly past as evidenced by the monumental Alexandrian library, for a man associated with brilliant towering civilizations like the ancient Egyptian and Songhai empires, organized societies that thrived in harsh and wild Africa, something must have happened to steal his thunder. What that is, is most probably the reason behind the de-Africanization of the African.

Brainwashing is a possible tool.

Explorers came to Africa primarily, it seems, to pave the way for faith. Faith brought education. Education involved much more than reading and arithmetic. It became a tool to set apart the ones who changed to the new faith and forged a brotherhood with the visitor, learning and accepting his ways. The man with the new education was in a different class and was a colleague to the visitor. He spoke differently. And when governments of the visitor came to partition the wild lands, the converts fought for the visitors.

Who then de-Africanized the African?

The African's trust in one who had no respect for trust was the former's undoing.

The subtle indoctrination that set him apart from his brother through the new education system worked against him then, as it still does. His conscience was compromised. Through association with the visitor, through his assumed superiority as one educated, our man, when the government of the visitor came to claim territory, had no choice but to join ranks with his mentor. He was effectively de-Africanized.

African. The present man. Still brilliant but carrying the burden of indoctrination. His brother is his business partner or he who can pay more for what is available. What is available is not necessarily the right thing. It's what fetches him a big chunk of ill-gotten gains. It's deals like these that are the reasons why civil wars—over crude oil and diamonds—are fought in Africa. Looking at the leadership of the so-called militias who maim, kidnap, rape, and kill their fellow villagers and/or communities, we see that they are men with education who often have lived for long periods in foreign countries. They have business ties with outsiders who fund them for these crimes. Often you find that such men have their immediate families safe in foreign cities while they carry out death sentences on their own people at home.

De-Africanization seems a well-thought-out scheme to keep Africa deeply involved in what appear to be eternal wrangles, but these are often well-orchestrated disasters so the unidentified and shadowy enemy can gain access to the resources that are available in a particular region. This then means that the de-Africanization is geared toward the looting of a continent's resources through hired local hands. Faith failed. The colonizers' governments failed. The citizens of the land have succeeded in the wholesale of looting of all the resources the foreigner ever wished for a price. The citizen in this case is the Trojan horse in his own city. The international criminal court in The Hague is playing the game of indictments and punishment for war criminals. Perhaps they should seek to indict the sponsors of the war criminals, because those are the real criminals.

De-Africanization is a false concept leveraged to downplay the hand of the actual criminals, corporeal entities who would do anything and everything for profit, including committing murder. The African is a small player satisfied with less, while much is sent home abroad for the real war instigators.

There are governments owned by other governments. There are leaders owned by crooked sponsors. There are humble folks who know the truth but have no voice against a machinery so complex that it owns the courts and the judges. That is the mess in which the African finds himself, and in fear of being exposed, he will dance as the master calls him to, for failure to do so will lead him to be ridiculed for his part in the hidden deals and cause him to fall from the sponsoring power, a fate so often orchestrated to perfection by hired whistle-blowers.

POETRY FROM SOUTH AFRICA

Morgana VientoLameculos

"Born and raised in South Africa, I have watched my country go from a safe place to a place of mayhem, crime, and political turmoil. And I have seen its transition from apartheid to a free democracy. With the latter came a free-for-all attitude—a system of riots and plunder, of racism and hate, of oppression and rape. We are governed by criminals, and the real people, the true citizens of this rainbow nation, are burdened and weighed down by the sorrowful governance that stops at nothing to undermine the peace, growth, and prosperity of our South Africa. I cannot turn a blind eye to the reality of what I see here on a daily basis. I will write of it and will not be silenced. I will speak out against what is happening here. Our people are murdered daily! Our people live in fear and in poverty amid unemployment and crime-ridden communities. Everyone is affected. There is not a person in my country who has not been affected (directly or indirectly) by crime.

"It is time for the world to see, to know ... It is time for change!"

CRY, MY BELOVED COUNTRY

Tears of blood staining your soil,
A history carved from skin and bones,
Wars and bombs no stranger here,
Children's names on bleak gravestones …
Your crimson skies reflect the fires
That burn within our souls.
Mountains high echo the cries
Of a lonely hyena's howl.
Your desert sands and silver moons,
A whisper of the silence heard.
Tear-filled rivers and daunting lagoons,
A witness carved into African soil.
Your heart is warm like the African sun.
Your blood runs wild, screams of freedom.
Your rhythms beat like a distant drum,
Yet with sadness you are overcome!
Cry, my beloved country;
Shed your tears for all the wrong.
Cry, my beloved Africa!
Write with your tears a brand-new song—
A song of hope, a song of peace.
Shout it out with voices strong,
For tears will dry and hope prevail.
Where love is abundant,
Hope and peace will never fail!

COLD AND LIFELESS

Drenched in blood,
This cold, lifeless body,
His cries not heard,
His pleas falling on deaf ears.
No mercy, not a grain
Of humane compassion.
His eyes dimming to the sight
Of his loved ones—dead!
Cold and lifeless,
His brutalized body,
Skin slashed open,
Cut to the bone!
Tears of sorrow
And deepest agony,
For he is incapable
Of protecting his family—
He, one man alone,
And they, six or more,
Armed with guns and knives,
Machetes glimmering,
Stained with the blood
Of those who died before him.

Her cries, the fear thumping
Like explosions in her chest:
"God have mercy on my children!"
Prayers and pleas not heard.
No, it becomes the war cry
For those who want to kill.
Over and over she is violated,
Raped, brutalized, tortured.
Evil is too mild a word
To describe the utter brutality
Fueled by a hatred so profound.
She glances, her body weak
And her heart thumping with pain,
The pain only a mother can understand,
The agony of seeing your child
Being sliced to pieces,
Throat slit, blood seeping
And soaking her face.
And she knows that this
Is her very last breath …
She looks frantically,
Still hoping that help will come,
And praying for her children,
Still innocent, too young to die!

Solemn silence follows the night.
Darkness creeps over him,
His eyes searching hopelessly
For a sound, a cry.
Silence is his only companion
As death creeps over him,
His tears mixed with blood,
His life fading with every heartbeat.
He mumbles her name,
Prays for her to be safe,
For their children to be unharmed.
As his last breath leaves his body,
Her heart stops beating too.
The children—cold and lifeless.
And the smell of blood
Is thick in the midnight air.

Cry for them, the families
That are slaughtered!
Cry for them, the children
Who know not of hate!
Cry for the mothers
Who see their children die!
Cry for the women—raped,
Brutalized, humiliated, killed!
Cry for the deaths of the innocents,
And cry for the injustices
To which so many prefer
To simply turn a blind eye,
A reality that too many still deny.

POETRY FROM UGANDA

Kabedoopong Piddo Ddibe'st was born, presumably, on February, 25, 1990, in Obem North village, Labongo Layamo Subcounty, Kitgum District, Uganda, East Africa. His parents are Duculina Lamunu and Gastony Odoki Nyamong, and he is the fourth of the six children born. He is a teacher of English and literature, besides being a literary writer. He has a number of published works both online and in anthologies.

SERVE THE POET

Serve the poet more papers—
the first ones are done—
then listen how to serve him.
Take the poet
to a big, a very big, hotel
where blood is served
(in the chapel of soldiers)
—then serve him not
any cup of coffee,
tepid, cold, or hot,
half-burnt or black burnt.
Serve him the cracking clips
of the blood-bathed quill,
and give him just a pot of paint
to dress the wounds.
Only unnursed wounds
smell worse than weeds.
Greater miracles are performed
by the barrel of the pen
than the guns have ever done.

Serve the poet more papers
with dog-eared pages,
overstained with perfect dirt:
life is not well shaped;
it has wounded lips,
like the lips of an abnormal godchild.
Take the poet
to a big, a very big, hotel
where diabetics are served
sucrose in the salt,
or salt in the sugar ...
Serve the poet chloroquine
to mend our broken shoes
(eaten by the teeth of nails on our beds),
for the healing power
of chloroquine lies in its bitterness;
once the bitterness is over,
the sickness is healed.

Serve the poet more papers,
for your silent lamentations
outnumber the seashore sands.
Only grieved words can describe;
words are sharper than swords.
Tears shed on papers are easier heard
than the thudding feet
of ten thousand swordsmen
marching for genocide
in the still of the night.
Serve him not the people's meat
but the barrel of the pen;
sit back in limbo, quiet,
on your bed of pain
as he surges the panting pus:
don't bite the hand that treats you.
Once the pus is pierced,
the pain is over.
And what is more—
the sick world is healed.

RUPING AND ANYADWEE

Ruping:

O beloved, I am your beloved man;
Ruping is your beloved lover,
Son of Luo, the son of Kakanyero.
I sing this love song for you,
The daughter of the lily,
The lily of the wet valley,
Anyadwee of Gulu Town.
The river between us
Roadblocks us from loving each other.
O my most beautiful rose,
The rose of the green valley,
A white man surpasses you with color. O!
Oh no! You are a white woman.
Ay! White rose in black skin.
I came to this sugarcane garden to work
And then pay your dowry;
I came this sugarcane garden
To work
And then marry you,
Little though they pay me,
The mangiest salary.
Our Akumu marriage must enter,

But one barrier stops me from loving you:
Your lovely sister wants me to marry you,
But your brothers hate our sweet love.
They want to break us apart.
Your lovely mom wants me to marry you,
But your father wants to cut off my neck
Because I am deeply in love with you.
He says I am not good enough to marry you.
He says he doesn't speak my language.
He says you don't know my language.
He says my tribe eats people.
He says my culture is barbaric.
Barbaric! Barbaric! Barbaric culture!
He says I don't have a Matooke plantation.
O, he says, I don't have a herd of cattle.
O, he says, I don't have an AK-47 for his rearing cattle.
O, he says, I don't look presentable.
O, he says, I am black charcoal:
"Ruping is as black as a well-burnt piece of charcoal!"
O my beautiful woman,
O my beautiful Anyadwee,
Must I miss a woman because of these objections he raises?

O no, my beloved, O!
My love for you is so natural,
My love for you is so emotional,
My love for you is so international.
My love for you is like God,
Everywhere, everywhere, my love!
Even if I don't have money,
Stay with me till I die.
True love never dies,
But the love for worldly things dies
And dies forever and evermore;
It fades away like a beautiful shadow!
Your name is a vase of roses,
Smelling of sweet perfume
From the Kenya highlands
Where the white settlers drove
The black laborers with whips.
Your eyes are a pair of stars;
Your beautiful legs are twin golds,
Glittering like the beauty of the pearl.

But my only worry is you might leave me—O!—
Under the pressure of your people,
Who say I don't belong to your tribe,
Who say I don't know your language.
But my love doesn't know any people.
My love doesn't know any race,
Be it black or white, yellow or green. O
My love doesn't mind any race. O
It is blind to those xenophobic ones.
Be it for a European, an Indian, or an African,
True love never ever discriminates. O!
Be it Australian, Japanese, or Chinese,
American or Aaaaaaaaaaaa!

My love never, ever underrates.
My love is not the apartheid policy.
I am a proud African.
You're my beautiful black beauty;
Your skin is the skin of shea nut oil,
Glistening like a dust of goldfish.

Anyadwee:

Ruping, my beloved man,
Look into my starry eyes.
I have something to tell you:
You are the joy of my life.
If they refuse our love,
I will fall dead before them.
I love you not for money.
I love you not for your tribe.
I love you not for your language.
I love you because you are my joy.
Money cannot buy love;
I will love you till I die.
My love for you will always be.
I love you not for your color.
I love you not for your race.
I love you not for your culture.
After all, I am an African girl.
I know how to cook *malakwang*
With nice-tasting rotten cowhides
Pasted with thick simsim.
I know how to dress like an Acholi woman,
With hems dragging on the ground.
I know how to kneel before your papa;
I know how to kneel before your mama,
With both knees stuck on the ground.

I will learn the Acholi language;
I will eat what you eat.
Don't leave me, my love,
Just because I don't belong to your tribe,
For true love springs from the heart,
From the depth of the heart,
Not from the depth of the tribe,
Nor from races, nor from languages of the world.

Ruping:

O my sweet, daughter of my mother,
My reverend mother-in-law,
Anyadwee, I love you
From the depth of my heart.
New moons come and die on my head
While I blow thee my best flute
And sing for you the loveliest song.
Many, many beautiful ones are dying for me,
But unluckily I have no more vacancies
In my heart, except the one for you,
Anyadwee the Beautiful One.
Who else is like you?
You have filled the missing chasm
My former wives left in my heart;
They could not understand me.
But now I have got you, O baby,
The daughter of Gulu Town.
They say the beautiful ones
Are not yet born,
But since beauty lies in the eyes
Of the beholder,
I behold that the most beautiful one
Is now born, and that is you, Anyadwee.

I came to this sugarcane garden
To work and then marry you.
My ancestral cattle have gone to Kotido;
Our cattle have gone to Kotido.
Cattle raiders came from the Far East
And kidnapped our cattle.
Now I feel the blowing dry winds
In the Acholiland.
If the cattle were there,
I would marry you with the whole kraal;
If granaries still stood on our compound,
I would marry you with the whole barns.
Daughter of the moon,
Ruping would have married you.
I came to this cement mine
To work and then marry you.
My mother wants to see you;
She wants me now to marry you.
I left Natasha the city girl
And followed you, Anyadwee.
You are not a woman of makeup,
Lipstick on the lips,
Eyeliner on the eyelashes,
Lucifer's claws on the fingers,
Miniskirt above the thighs.
You are a simple village girl.
You are not like Natasha the city girl
With a python skin.
You are a simple village girl,
Well-mannered, sweet-tongued,
The host of innumerable, ceaseless guests.
O daughter of the lily,
The valley of the red roses,
Love me the way I am,

The poor orphan child.
Mother died in the Great War
Between the regime and the rebels.
My real father died in the Great War
Between the regime and the rebels.
Anyadwee, hear my flute.
The child of a poor man
Lives by his own hands.
I want you to be mine, baby girl.
Will you marry me, Anyadwee,
Daughter of the moon?

Anyadwee:

Yes, I will marry you, my beloved one.
True love comes from the heart,
Neither from the west nor from the east,
Neither from the north nor from the south,
But from the heart of the heart
Of the two in love.
Neither from the mother nor from the father,
Neither from the sisters nor from the brothers,
But from the depth of the hearts
Of the two in love.
Don't enter into two other people's issue.
I will marry you, my dove.
Turn a deaf ear to rumormongers.
The clouds are pregnant with golden rains.
The winds of love are blowing.
Take me away, O beloved.
Take me away where nature sways gladly.
Take me away among the roses,
The dandelions, the lilies, and the golden marigold,
And show me love. And kiss me.

I am tired of hearing artificial nature.
I am sick of noise, smoke, tear gas, and riots.
Take me far from the madding crowd
To the green mountainsides,
Where pastures bloom for the sheep.
I am tired of the sickening city life,
Watching orphans on the bare streets beg,
Watching blood of the innocent flow;
I am tired of the stinking city life,
Full of nasty, weird, and disgusting life.
Take me away from the muddy roads
Full of potholes and job-seekers,
Of mothers and children caught
In the hungry jaws of wheel killers.
Take me away from these dirty games
Full of lies, murders, and violence,
Of politricksters, assassins, and rioters.
I want to feel the cool winds
Blowing on the head of the mountain
Where waters run deep with warm love
Like in the Garden of Eden.
The son of the king,
My handsome prince,
Ruping, do you love me,
And won't you leave me, O?

Ruping:

May I drop dead, my princess,
If ever I drop you like a rejected stone.
I swear by my dead mother,
Whose breast I sucked till my teeth were full,
That I, Ruping, won't leave you.
Many men have conned you

And dropped you like a rejected stone.
They left the white ants on the anthill;
You are the white ant they left:
Your skin is like the wings of white ants.
Your neck resembles the neck of an Abino jar.
Your eyes are a multitude of stars;
Your teeth sparkle like diamond dust.
Sadly, truly,
Many men have deceived you
With the greatest lies of their lives,
But they have dumped you like rubbish
Into the dustbin of their history …
Men are like women;
You never can trust them with your heart to keep.
But I trust you, Anyadwee.
They say all men are the same,
But I disagree with them all;
All men are not the same …
All men are not the same, but equal,
So my love for you will never change.

A river doesn't flow back to its source, Anyadwee;
You are now very ripe, and nature must take its course.
You are the brightest star at night,
In whom my broken heart delights;
You are the heaven on the earth:
I will be with you till my last breath.
I will take you away from the city,
To my people in the local community.
I will take you to the mountainside,
Where we will play hide-and-seek:
I seek you. O, when you hide,
I will kiss your dimpled cheeks
And make love bloom in the wild,
Where no forbidden fruits grow white.

Anyadwee:

I love your love song, darling;
You're killing me here softly …
Tarry not. Take me now home,
Where I see your papa and mom,
Where I see the sky, blue sky,
And where we become one, you and I,
Till I become a loving mommy
And you become a loving daddy.
Hold my hands and take me away.
Take me forever, now and today.

RUPING AND ANYADWEE
(The Ugly Ones Are Already Born)

Soft words are patiently said:
Good things are for those who wait,
For the beautiful ones are not yet born.
So I patiently waited for tomorrow's presence,
But those were sweet soft words of the afterlife;
All I have ever seen is tomorrow's absence.
Soft words soften hard hearts,
The treasure in my box of chocolate.
Did you ever see my brown box of memory?
The whole box was stolen while I slept,
Snoring on my bed of thorns like a toddler.
You must have seen my Gwele;
It is a bed made of bagged cotton wool
And bundle of sticks hard enough to break your ribs.
That bundle of sticks, I crossed them on the bed.
Soft words really soften hard hearts.
"Don't worry, Ruping. Women are like waters.
You never can finish them all!
They are as many as the stars of heaven.
All women are the same!"
They often comfort me like a crying child
Whose loaf of bread has fallen on the soil;
They make me wonder if they have tasted all women,
That all women are the same!

That the beautiful are not yet born,
And spilled milk cannot be scooped back up.
All they say is like a flying flag
Of a Mickey Mouse independence.
"Are the ugly ones already born?" I ask them.
"Anyadwee is one of the beautiful ones already born!
If this is not so, when will the beautiful ones be born?
You mean to say they're born if I am dead?"
I ask them, and their mouths are now tall,
Like the beaks of marabou birds,
With burning anger running through their spines.
They are my clansmen after all.
I must rise up tomorrow as if I am mad
And travel to Kampala, city of the people,
And search for my lost wife in the city squares,
Until I bring her back home;
If not, then how will I endure the cruel mockeries
Of my kinsmen, age mates, and village men?
How will I, Ruping, son of Okayo-Tobi, live here
In this jealous village of Kakanyero? How?
How will Ruping stand the fierce roaring laughter
Of the village women from Kakanyero and Kakamega
Who come in quest of waters from the well
Dug by my forefathers ages ago in Kakanyero?
And they are to walk many miles away back home
Because their lousy government failed to bore
Mere holes—boreholes—in this region,
While they gallop for taxpayers' money
And bend their funny heads, extending
Some nonhumanistic, non compos mentis,
Unprofessional, unconstitutional,
Unstoppable, combatant, and neocolonialistic presidential age limit,
While village women leave their homeless houses
And walk through bushes in search of clean drinking waters:

Leaving their houses before their husbands are done,
Before the last cockcrow like Samaritan women,
Before their babies wake up hungry
And begin demanding breast milk
From their flat, milkless chests
Because foods don't satisfy them in the first place.

The clansmen gathered their gray heads against me,
With thousands of false accusations, choices,
And hidden intrigues seen in their red eyes.
They have chosen seven virgin women for me!
I wonder if virgin mothers are there.
They say I must choose one from their choices,
Or take them all at once to replace Anyadwee,
Who is gone already, they say:
Gone, never to return, like the stubborn new colonialists.
They say she is in the safe custody of Mugaga the rich man.
I wonder if there is any safe custody,
Because they remind me of my very police;
You never can be safe in their hands,
Even if you were imprisoned like Mandela.

No, I will not tarry about.
I will wake up tomorrow with machetes in my hands
And will never listen to their words of the dead.
And I will give them the biggest surprise of their lives,
Not just a surprise, but a great wonder:
I will prove them all wrong,
If they think their artificial love will conquer me.
My love for Anyadwee is a natural spring of living water.
I will let them marry their artificial virgin women
Whose beauty is created by makeup
And let them know that true love conquers all
And that true love is not forced;
I will marry who I want,
Like the government kills who they want most.
Yes, I will travel to the city on foot tomorrow,
Though my legs will swell like those of Oliver Twist,
With machetes in my naked hands,
To gather back what belongs to Caesar.
They say I lack elderly respect for them
And that I think childish thoughts,
But they with their elderly thoughts
Forget to remember my right to choices.
They threaten to excommunicate me
If I break their mouths and follow my ways
By not choosing their ready-made choices.
No, I follow my heart;
Life is what you choose, to be or not to be.

No
Weapons formed against my love shall prosper;
I am my love's defender. She is my world …
The girl bloody mosquitoes bit me for,
The girl I endured bitter cold nights for,

The girl I postponed sleep for,
The girl I refused to eat food for,

The girl I risked my whole life for …
I will never, ever succumb to their hollow-bottomed threats;
My heart is my king, and my fear is my enemy.

Where my heart is, is where my treasure is,
So come elephant rains or flames of sunshine;
No cartons of traditional and political threats
Shall frighten me away from my love of life.
I will fry my groundnuts tonight
And roast my long cassava, and pack them up,
And fill up my long umbilical-corded calabash with water,
And have all my safari necessities ready to go
Before the people of Kakanyero are awake
At the red dawn of Lakana.
And then I will rush to face the wildcat in the city
That catches people's chickens at night,
That has bribed Obina with five cents
To lure and turn the head of Anyadwee from me.
Obina will take the share of the price too,
For accepting to be used as a cat's paw.

Still, soft words are said to win my heart of stone.
They say many moons have passed now
And that foreign girls are stubborn;
They pack all your things in secret
And leave you a broken wall of Jericho.
Yes, sometimes I don't doubt that
That could be brilliant reasoning;
I hear they conspire to sacrifice my Anyadwee
To the hungry gods of their forefathers.
They say secretly that she is a slave girl.
A slave girl?
Let them try! They will milk a male wildcat!
They will fan the flames of Third World war!
But I know Anyadwee from A to Z;
She is a daughter to Balidina Lakang
And Jack Lumoro.
She is born of Kakamega,
The neighbor of Kakanyero.
She is not a spiritual slave in a spiritual prison.
She is freeborn, not born with the side rib;
Differences should not make a difference.

December 17, 2017

RUPING AND ANYADWEE
(Love Confession)

It got into my twin eyes,
Opened the gate of my heart,
Captured my mind,
Imprisoned my soul
Like an incorruptible virus,
Beat out food appetite,
And canceled my night's sleep …
If I filled my sleepless nights
With rainbows of dreams,
Engraved your holy name
On the tablets of my heart,
Gave its pulsating rhythms …

It devoured my flesh
Like a hungry lion,
Got into my bone marrow,
Consumed my little fat
Like a dry season wild bushfire,
And left me in a skeletal suit;
Got deep into my heart,
Created a chasm there,
And increased the missing fever.
And left me helpless.
There's a hole in my heart

Only you can fill;
I am sick without you.
People talk rubbish behind my back
And say our love is blind,
But they're blind to see
That love lies in the heart
Of the holder,
Let alone beauty …

It intensifies the enmity
Between darkness and light.
Some friends unfriended me.
Relatives say I have gone mad.
Sometimes I don't disagree with them;
Love is but a whole madness.
My mind refuses to think
Outside the coat yard
Of your colorful world,
All it maps in its huge
Central processing unit
Is your beautiful picture.

I am in love. Confession:
You're the pillar of my life.
If you fall down,
I will be worse than
A face without a nose.
Your beauty glitters like gold;
They say not all that glitters is gold,
But you're a glittering bit of gold yourself.
I am an iron filing.
You're a magnet;
You've magnetized my mind,
Like the yellow sun

Twists the head of a sunflower,
And turns it in its directions
In the phototropism of your diamond teeth …

Don't resist. My love advances for you.
Some African kings resisted
The coming of the white man.
Surrender to my love advances,
Like the converts who accepted
To be martyred at Namugongo shrine.
Anyadwee, do you hear my love flute?
Daughter of the moon,
Do you hear me whistling my hands,
Making you my love confession?

Hurry up. Come down to
The bed of my heart,
And clean up the mess of life;
Colonize and loot my golden heart
Like the colonial masters did.
I love you like African rulers love thrones,
Like some women love money.
Every queen needs a king;
Be my queen. I'll be your king.

Please, I beg:
Come into my hollow heart,
Fill up the blank space,
Keep me in your prison,
And deny me access
To the forests of women
Outside the gate of my heart;
Let your love abduct me
Like Joseph Kony's
And Museveni's love affairs.
Draw me to the altar of love,
And burn your love incense
Into my gazelles of nostrils.
Some fall in love, and others fall out of love,
But keep me in the custody of your love.
My feet were restless for ages,
Like dry season he-goats,
Searching for my missing rib,
But now that I have got you,
Never will I fall in love again,
Let alone look any further.
So, give me a reason to live
Without your love defining
The meaning of my life,
O daughter of the moon.

December 29, 2017

RUPING AND ANYADWEE
(My Husband Sleeps with His Back Turned to Me)

In my house,
There are two women:
Me and my husband.

My mother-in-law and
My father-in-law
Prepare a black cock
And a black goat,
Cut their necks
And sacrifice them
And appease the angry ancestors,
Let them drink the blood,
And bless my husband
With one that irrigates
The sky with urine.
Let them soften the ghost
That sleeps
In the body of my husband.

My in-laws,
Your son is diseased.
He suffers from the sickness
That turns men's backs
To their married wives.
Your son has no shadow,
No shadow of the head;
Maybe a witch has caught
And bottled up the shadow of his head.

Your son lies down
Like the bull-testicled pumpkin;
He lies down like a corpse,
He sleeps in the evening
Together with the chicken
And wakes up in the morning
Together with the sun.
Your son's body needs
To be repaired;
It has some fault.

Why does Ruping,
My husband,
Who is your son,
Sleep like a python
That has swallowed an elephant alive?
Why does he sleep
Like a buffalo of laziness?
Why does he sleep
Like a lifeless log
Where a homeless monkey squats to sleep?

Mother of my husband,
Rush to help your son.
Two women don't share a house;
My husband and I are like co-brides,
Two women in one house.
My husband hurls insults
Beginning with his mother-in-law,
His father-in-law,
Dogs, chicken, goats, and things.

My husband speaks a woman's words
And sleeps like a pregnant mother
Who is about to deliver twins.
He sleeps arrogantly
Like a stubborn ox
That does not want to dig.
With his legs turned to my head,
He lies like a narrow black box
For tucking a corpse.

He says he does not want games,
That he does not want disturbances,
That he does not want a troublesome woman
Like me, Anyadwee,
A village woman
Whose head is a stone—
Primitive, savage, and barbaric
In her ways of walking
And talking …

Many moons have passed
Since the sweet honeymoon.
Ruping refused customary marriage.
Ruping refused Acholi marriage.
He refused to crawl
Into the house of his mother-in-law,
Saying that it is a barbaric marriage,
That he would rather pick up a rope
And hang himself
Than crawl on his knees
Like a baby learning to walk.

What troubles me
Is not his refusal
To have the customary marriage.
It is his manner of sleeping
That is directionless
And provocative.
I want Ruping
To trouble me,
To play with me,
To knock my head,
To beat me
When my body itches.
My joy comes from pain,
The sweet husbandry pains.
I only sleep well when I am beaten …
But my husband is mean.
He does not have the rage
Under his fingernails to scratch my face.
He cannot trouble me,
And yet I need him to.
He does not tickle me.
He looks at me

Out of the corners of his eyes.
He does not want to nudge me;
This house is a graveyard.

My in-laws,
Did I marry your son
To be wallpaper
Or Christmas decoration?
When did I become
A TV or a radio
To be heard or watched
In this compound?
There is no child cry!

I have become a picture
Nailed on the wall for visitors.
I have become a byword
And a laughingstock
For the fierce laughter of village women.

My mother,
The wife of my father,
My father,
The husband of my mother,
Do you hear your daughter's
Song of lamentation?

If I talk,
Saying that the Padwat opened
The teeth of a goat,
That I have many mouths—
Mouth for gossip,
Mouth for true lies,
Mouth for half-truths,

Which are total lies …
But Mother,
Is this how Father behaved
When he eloped with you
From his father's compound?
Who is he that is not envious?
Envy catches us all;
Even Jehovah is envious.
My envy is healthy.
I need the cry of a child,
A child of mine.
Women marry good men,
But my man burns my heart.
Why do I have to sew the baby carrier
Without the baby?

Ruping,
My husband, sleeps
With his back turned to me
As if I am his mother's daughter!
The son of my father-in-law sleeps arrogantly
With his legs turned to my head.
My husband sleeps arrogantly;
His hunchback is ever turned
Adjacent to my face.
He snores with saliva
Like a nameless newborn baby.
Neighbors complain
That his snores disturb their children's sleep.
They always wake up prematurely
Like a stillborn death.

Mother,
Speak to me.
This is not suing the son of man.
Speak to me, Mother.
Am I my husband's sister
That he sleeps with his back
Directly proportional to me?

A VOICE IN THE DARK

Africa,
Your righteous disorders
Break my heart.
Cowards are brave
With guns in their hands
In your bleeding ancestral lands.
You once blamed the white man
For auctioning your black children
To the plantations overseas,
Down the Mississippi River,
But at this moment of silence,
I bow my head in crying shame
And salute your bright follies,
For you can neither weep nor feel.
Your heart is blunt and numb.
You can't feel your own shame.
You can't blame yourself,
You who call yourself
The mother of all humankind,
For selling your own children
Down the running Nile River.
I am ashamed of you calling me
Your beloved cultured son.

Africa,
Your righteous evil
Gouges out the eye of humanity.
You brave cowards!
Cowards are brave
With tools in their hands.
The world is a webbed cage;
We're mere flightless birds
With short-cut wings,
With unheard birdsongs,
With blunted tongues:
Only unheard echoes of dirges.
The bond of the nations
Is impotent like castrated bulls
And can't fertilize a single peace.
What she does best is sit back
And watch the new faith
Of modern slavery
Trump over guiltless humanity.

Africa,
Your rising darkness
Overshadows me
With clouds of heart pain,
For the bullets in the heads
Of children, men, and women …
That's what cowards do!
Strong men don't fight wars,
But against wars rather,
Not for injustice,
But against injustice …
Where are your men,
With pairs of buttocks on their chests,
Who fought against the scramblers?

Where are the men
With thick heads and hearts
Who stood still and looked
Apartheid in the eyes
And loudly and boldly said no?
And where are the brave men
Who returned the cultural loot
From the white man's land?
Are there no more brave men
With such chests, heads, and hearts
In this land of black slavery?
I stand tall against your wiping arms!
Africa, if you are my mother,
Then don't call me your son anymore.
Your name is my crying shame.
Your remaining children are assassins,
Power hungry and money thirsty;
Your human markets are full
With human commodity.
Your back wounds will never heal
As you preach life but kill.

THE PEARL

The pearl still bleeds well.
The futile flag still flies
In the gun-smoked air.
Crawling and weaning
From aftermath colonial breasts,
A baby, they say, that stands
Can now be given hard foods
Like bones and nails to chew.
The false teeth fall off,
But the pearl still bleeds well.
The flag still follows the cross,
And the head that wears the crown
In the womb of the realm,
Counts his hundredth birthday.
Puppets still play the clowns.
The pearl still bleeds well:
Technical know-who
Overshadows technical know-how.
Chest bones are still visible
From thousands of miles away.
They still pluck the guns
To play the mother drum
As they lick the national cakes
Flowing down the stems

Of their overeaten hands.
The pearl still bleeds well;
Refugees in camps are okay
With the meager meals each day.
Nothing to worry about here:
Let the world look the other way
Like they always do
When fires of slavery spark off here.
Let them not worry at all;
It is just the beauty
I read in their faces
As River Nile flows back
To its source in Lake Victoria.

BALLAD OF THE FIVE FOOLISH VIRGINS

I.
Five foolish virgins, once upon a time,
Sent to dry grains, to dry wet grains;
Five foolish virgins wisely did combine,
Spread the grains, couldn't see the rains.
(Couldn't see this could bring some pains.)

II.
Clouds, dark and pregnant, soon came.
Grains on the bare rocks, the girls with some boys.
The rains came with furious sword and flame.
They played hide-and-seek, sowing seeds with toys.
(Fish love, blind love! O little coys.)

III.
The eldest of all had the strongest voice,
A voice to make all play far away.
The little girls had no other choice
But to follow where the corpse would go play.
(At the end of the day, we all must pay.)

IV.

Off to play, out to play, little fellows,
With those heathen cowboys, young and gay.
Friendly matches—matches in death rows.
We little 'uns got a lot of games to play.
(One frog spoils the whole water source, pray!)

V.
Rap! Rap! Were the legs of rains on the grounds
Washing grains for food far away?
Tap! Tap! Were the rains with silly sounds
Wetting grains of girls in the broad day?
(Since twelve o'clock, the girl still did play.)

VI.
Ngio! Ngio! Were the grains on the bald rocks
Dried enough, brittle enough, to be collected?
But these rains cut like the teeth of mattocks.
Rok! Rok! Were the rains soon started?
(At two o'clock, the girls still played.)

VII.
Pat! Pat! With their long snakes of ropes,
Good little girls still skipped so high,
Their heads touched and troubled raindrops
From the blankets of the world in the sky.
(At four o'clock, the good girls still skipped by.)

VIII.
Wak! Wak! More incessant rains had soon begun.
Still good girls in the rains played too much,
And back forth they couldn't anymore run.
O these rains, nothing could ever touch!
(At six o'clock, good girls still played in a rush.)

IX.
Tac! Tac! Hailstones soon started to pour.
Cold like death, they really did fall,
Striking to startle someone to remember;
Oh, Akumu soon remembered, reminded them all.
(Too late to hurry; grains gone to rains call.)

X.
Down, down, bend down, virgin girls;
In your calabashes, in your woven baskets,
Pick the wet grains before the night falls.
No calabashes? No baskets? Use your pockets.
(No pockets? Rush back home like Newton's rockets.)

XI.
Good girls, run before the end of the rush hour.
Mother's pacing like her house's burning;
Run to the best of your youthful power.
Chase the day! Keep your worlds turning
(Till father's fury and fire stop burning).

XII.
Empty-handed—Kwet! Kwet!—the girls returned;
Except Akumu, they'd all gotten a dirty trick:
Some bad boys their baskets overturned.
Some bad boys, like monsters ugly and black.
(Sleep with your mother-in-law under water. Bubbles strike back.)

XIII.
Father's got a lie tester. He couldn't believe.
Whip swung in his right hand, ready to swish,
"Little minds do little deeds." Mother gave him relief.
She wanted his fury and fire to be an off switch.
(Mother's love plays big games in the fury pitch.)

XIV.
Here, Father's fury and fire boiled greater!
Little virgins, we're all players at best,
But for your mother's pity, you'd see a whip better!
We all must admit truths for the sake of the jest.
(Duty at hand, hands on duty than the rest.)

XV.
Go gentle, Father. Go gentle and cozy;
Whips don't whip out the wrongs.
Wrongs, like spilled milk, can't be collected. Worse when tipsy.
Hear me, Akumu. Hear my wounded songs!
(We overdid an overdose on our rights for too long.)

XVI.
Father, forgive us. Just go gentle.
Mother, I take refuge behind you. Speak for us. Speak!
We met some good demons with cattle
And really overplayed that hide-and-seek.
(Little did we know, our mud-walled house overleaks.)

XVII.
We met devils face-to-face in the wild
That promised to marry us after the sweet taste,
But our hearts now yearn for more, wilt with guilt,
Because the devils surely won the test.
(And here, lost sheep stand to embrace the bitter taste.)

XVIII.
Yes, little girls, the devil really tempts,
But, you see ... to be tempted is not to sin;
Only you wrought my heart with contempt.
"It is written" would have made you win!
(Once the angels sin, twice the devils win.)

XIX.
The devil tempts feeble hearts and wins,
But Mother's love wins twice with forgiveness.
Father's heart, a chasm where fire oft burns,
Soon is healed by a touch of loveliness.
(When fire catches water, fire dies.)

XX.
Go, my girls. Next time be careful;
Don't die for your unknown desire:
Be heedful, be punctual, be helpful,
For your mother's love has extinguished my fire.
(Fury and fire end in Mother's love's desire.)

CHESS GAME

Cunning is the head
That wears the crown
In the game of chess,
In the heart of the realm.
The invincible king,
Sitting unmoved by fear
Of the future ghosts,
Crosses the check unchecked
In his territorial zone—
With diplomatic terror
In the elimination method,
With catastrophic terror
In the displacement method—
Of the rules of the game,
In the bedroom politics
Of the queen and king,
Romancing the chessboard
In whiteness of their teeth,
But redness of their hearts.

No stalemate in this game.
You lose and live, or die.
Don't speak liberty;
Don't speak majority rule.
Speak gun rule rather,
And then live forever.
No pawn crosses this red
Carpet laid for the king.
Don't raise your head.
Don't open your mouth.
Move like a dumb shadow.
Move hurriedly and worriedly.
This is a beautiful dangerous
Zone paved with glittering gold.
The Catholics of commanders,
Armed rooks patrol
The royal castellation
As the tall clock chimes;
Knights of constellations,
With instruments of immorality,
On the autocratic black mass,
And combatted bishops of soldiers
In the diagonal city square
Of the chapel, eat with cups
And drink blood with plates,
Waiting for more sacrificial blood
In the temple of debate.
The chessboard is the king's.

THE VIRGIN RAVEN

Once upon a blessed time, beauty was born
Where shining stars, moons, and suns shone;
A beauteous raven was born in heaven,
And from heaven she came like a bolt of levin,
Down, as a rose, on my poor planet heart.
"Blessed be God," said he, "for he made death,
That I may live forever and die no more!"
This raven, beautiful as ne'er before,
A dark continent, a black veil had she.
Charming princess born unborn for me
In beauty white, in virtue charcoal black.
O raven rapped, tapped her wings back.
Her beauteous feathers sloughed behind
As she fled to the island of hell beyond.

SONG TO THE GUEST

Eat not barehanded with death, thou guest,
Like when days are sweet and full of praise,
Lest thou sweetly go down humbly to rest.
With bitter lips, awake, thou old guest, always.
Sleep with one of your eyes open like hell's gate,
Walking down Despond Slough where zombies rise,
Where only love wholly conquers black hate;
Walk with thy eyes wide-widthed and very wise.
Be not worldly wise dying a blind death.
If eating with wet deaths, use long forks,
Thyself in the jaws of death, seeking breath.
Be wise and old if you're young, thou folks.
Many in mournful numbers went with venoms.
Ask heavens if deaths resemble phantoms.

ANIMAL MEETING

Chapter 1

Once upon a time, all the jungle animals were called for a meeting to discuss the tragedy that had befallen the jungle where they lived. The tragedy was a long, waterless life. The heavens had withheld their waters because humankind had cut mournful numbers of trees in the forests for their selfish gain. All the animals wanted water to keep them alive. Some of the animals had started to cut the arms of creeping plants to get water. It should be noted that besides experiencing a flood of drought for a long time, they had had their waters stolen by human beings on certain occasions to feed their betrayers, the domesticated animals, without the knowledge or consent of their master, King of the Jungle, the fiercest and strongest man of the jungle, His Excellency the Lion. Besides, cases of allegation had been recorded that Honorable Rhino the Piggy, who was the chairman of this meeting, was accused of receiving brides of milk in exchange for the waters that were in the dams and lakes far and near. He denied the allegations and said they were fabricated lies meant to soil his clean name. He was called Mr. Clean too—because he had no hair that would make other animals look ugly.

All these water sources were in the vicinity of the home of humankind. Immediately the lakes and dams ran dry. Humankind started using boreholes, which they were very keen to ensure tight security so that no wild animals would touch even a drop of water from them.

Before the meeting started, some mouthy member animals had already started giving their opinions in heavy low voices from down here. Some had already started giving salt and bars of soap and lumps of sweets for votes. They thought it was an election meeting, or a caucus, or something of that nature.

The meeting was supposed to kick off at exactly 8:00 a.m. and last until the time they resolved the matter. All the other animals had arrived in or on time except Mr. Hare the Wise.

After waiting for a pretty long time, like for half an hour, the Lion, the king of the jungle, who also arrived late to the meeting, grabbed the Canopy of Honor from Honorable Rhino undisputedly, like Napoleon did from the head of the pope, and wore it on his own head, all by himself.

He quickly, without a second thought, appointed Mr. Tiger as the chief whip, Mr. Zebra as the secretary, Squirrel as the timekeeper, Warthog as the welfare master, and himself as Everything. The rest of the members formed the silent audience. After the appointments, he asked all members to introduce themselves. The introduction was done by every individual attendee.

Without a waste of time, the Lion cleared his heavy throat and roared in addressing the audience: "My ladies and gentlemen, I take this opportune moment to ... Hey! Silence, every soul ... Every stubborn soul, silence!"

There were no female animals at the meeting, only male ones. This outburst surprised the animals. Lion tried to quell the mournful noises himself, but the crowd was too much for his bearing. He ordered the chief whip, who whipped up the stubborn members to warm up. Unpeaceful order was restored under the baobab tree, swallowed up by the mournful numbers of males. It should be noted that the Lion prohibited the females from attending the meeting, saying that they had no sense in their words. They should be cooking in their kitchens like kitchen police. The animals looked blankly at one another as the Lion looked at them squarely in their faces, unapologetically. Who said Excellencies apologize?

"Your Excellency," said Warthog the Toothed, "you have already denied the female animals from attending this meeting, but you forgot you did it. Though your most righteous confabulation—sorry, I mean discourse—shows that they are here in the meeting, which is what made the audience grunt. They're very sorry, Your Excellency, but you can continue. Please, sir."

"Ladies and gentlemen, I was saying that I take this wasteful time to welcome all of you to this meeting of its kind," said Lion, divided between annoyance and amazement. "Abrupt as the meeting is, I would like to record my displeasure with some of you in what will go down in posterity as a significant event, that those brainless things should know who I am. Who said My Excellency makes mistakes? Nobody. Desist! And secondly, as the white man says: 'Time is money, but fools waste both time and money and lose themselves.' So as the chairman and Everything, I decree that any good time waster will see what the monkey saw in the garden of peas. He will receive punishment. Lethal punishment. I am the law, and the law is the Lion."

He made them sing his words as a chorus, in unison:

> The law is the Lion.
> The Lion is the law.
> Nobody's above the law
> But the Lion of Zion.

Afterward, the angry animals were pacified with sweets and local brews to quell their conflagration of anger. Silence and peace returned.

"First of all, thank you for your noise, that fantabulous chorus," said the Lion. "Secondly, this meeting was called for, for a damn strong reason. Water! Everybody say, '*Water is life!*' Everybody!"

Everyone repeated what he said.
"Yes, good pupils! That is the reason. Water! I want to hear your suggestions about what we can do to restore the lost glory of abundance as it was before in this jungle."

Hands were seen raised up for suggestions.
One animal was pointed at.

"First of all, I apologize on behalf of my colleagues for what happened to you, Your Excellency," said Mr. Fox. "I suggest that we change the course of River Nile to let it pour its waters into our dam and lakes."

"Null and void," somebody shouted from amid the audience.
The argument continued. Some animals concurred. Other animals rejected the view blankly.

At one point, Mr. Hare arrived in his black waistcoat, dragging his feet on the ground to get everybody's attention. In his hand there was a bottle of wine.

"You can never find anyone who plays dirty games as nicely as I do. The rest are fake. Too many fake animals. Too many fake kings in the jungle. Too many fake skins and hides," said Hare the Drunk. He was always like that, always drunk for any sensitive meeting.
Someone called him to sit down and to stop making unnecessary noise for the animals. He first refused to sit down, saying he was not born lame and was not too lame to stand up. He preferred standing up to sitting down like a malnourished baby. He sat down unpunished. Some animals said he had amulets around his waist. Some said he was just blessed for the moment. Other moments would be for his punishments.

Another animal gave his view that they would do better to pray for rain to fill the dam. Of all the views given, this one was considered the least, as some argued that no talk talks better than the talker and no deed does better than the doer.

"I salute you all, dear jungle clan," said Hare the Drunk.
"All protocols observed. Don't punish the wise to please the fools. I mean, for my part, I would say that all the animals, tomorrow, by 8:00 a.m. sharp, should be here. Why? Take it or leave it, but I suggest that tomorrow we should dig up a well of our own! Some of you are laughing at me because I am drunk, but drunkenness is better than ugliness. You see this red, red wine some stubborn authority gave me in return for my precious votes that led to his four consecutive wins—undisputedly. Unquestioned. Unrelentingly. Unparliamentarily. Unrealized and all the uns. I have taken four different bottles now consecutively, too, in honor of that which is horrible. One bottle from the convent. Straight from the cemetery. Sorry, from what? From the … the sacristy. Meaning I drink only Roman wines … wines from Rome. The blood of Christ in remembrance of Holy Week. Most of the bottles I drank are from a higher authority I told I would not vote for anymore next time should he give me any more wine for my one vote. Wines enslave the drinker. They are like Satan, giving with the left hand but demanding with the right hand. They—" A fit of coughing dug his throat. "But I have realized that these are bottles of laughter. Bottles of mockers. Bottles of burdens. Bottles of chains. Just a bond of bondage. Me and the authority. Me and the bottles. Me and the votes. Me and the sentry. The more I drink, the more I am laughed at. Unfortunately, in the first place, some of you laughing should be not be looked at; your beauty stinks, like you, Warthog, with angry projected teeth. Why laugh when you yourself are a thing of laughter? Tomorrow I will be sober, but you—you, Mr. Warthog, will still remain ugly. If any pageantry for the ugly ones were to be held here, you would take the position of king of the ugly. You are so ugly that you need to be looked at for money on stage! Why have the guns to play the drums?"

"Ha-ha-ha. Enough, Mr. Hare the Wise. I was not laughing at you but the fly that passed by the corner of my mouth," said Mr. Warthog the Toothed.

All animals, convinced, started nodding their heads in acceptance of the words and work the following day. At that point, the Lion dismissed the assembly of animals, saying that they would meet the following day for the digging up of the well. All animals were to come with all necessary tools to work together for the new well. They all went back home happily in preparation for the next day's work.

Chapter 2

Four weeks later, the need for water had become intense. The frequent postponements seemed to have done more harm than good. News had it that four young ones of Mr. Antelope were found dead in the house under a mysterious circumstance that was believed to have been caused by starvation: both lack of water to drink and food to eat. Mr. Hare had frequented the palace for assistance, but every time in vain. What Hare did best was to provoke actions while he stood aside and watched others do things. He needed the king to hold another meeting. He wanted the members to stop talking and start doing something. The king seemed to be sitting on matters arising as soon as they arrived on his table. Hare arrived at the palace when the maids had just finished preparing a variety of delicious foods for the king. As the food dishes were uncovered, the gatekeeper was opening the gate for Hare to enter the palace.

"Our ancestors," prayed the prayer maid, as the king smiled, "come and bless this food, for it is your gift that the royal family is about to eat, in the name of …"

"The people whom you oppress. Amen," said Mr. Hare as he entered the royal dining hall. "Your Highness, I beg. I am sorry for this intrusion,

but your dog outside there said I should greet you. I beg you awake from your sleep, Your Majesty. I beg you to know that that food is the bodies of the oppressed, and that cup of wine you have on the table is the cup of the tears of the oppressed. While you eat and drink here, they starve and die there. Their sorrows are your joys. Look, I even wonder now if you are a true king of ours. Look at that coat, that woven or knitted foreign cap of yours. True kings are not funnel-footed like you. Now back to business. Last time—if my memory is right, three weeks ago now—you said the animals needed to dig up well so that we could save the lives of our dying children and of us too, but it seems you don't mind anymore how the people are falling dead in this kingdom. I know I suggested that. But nobody seems to care about all this stuff except dollars.
"I beg that you do something about the situation. It is time we stopped wasting time and did something in earnest. You can't sit back and watch the situation leap from frying pans into fires while all you do is enjoy seeing the people die."

"You have got no right to talk to the king like that. Shut up, you little bastard," said the bodyguard, trying to arrest Hare, who'd forced himself out of the hands of the guard.

"Let him talk. I want to hear his case," said the king.

"Why stop me now? Was my mouth made for passing out excrement? Leave adults' issues to adults, you son of a dog. If all you do best is sit on the throne and order things to happen like miracles, then Hare the Drunk won't attend your nonsense again. But before that, I would like to say I will be available for work tomorrow, unless you don't want water dug. I beg you awake from your sleep, My Beloved Majesty. I rest my case."

"The king doesn't sleep. The king is always awake," replied King Lion. His guards were on a standby, outfitted with their tight royal weapons.

"Postponement made the lizard not build his house," added the Hare as he left the palace, still talking to himself.

"The king knows!" replied the king.
It was a custom that when the king said "The king knows," it meant that the speaker could stop the dialogue there at the point it pad reached. Mr. Hare continued talking to himself outside the palace.
"That is the way they are. They promise you everything but do nothing about it. Anyway, I will wait tomorrow as he says. The king knows! King, come. See, your dog is wandering alone out here. He's the man of the people? Even keeping his dog alone defeats him. Fake king!"

The sun had risen up in the cloudless sky. All the animals assembled themselves under the huge baobab tree as usual to decide on what was to be done. The Tiger, who was in charge of security, arrived at Mr. Hare's home at 11:00 a.m. with some other animals. He and his men had not yet stepped well on the compound when Mr. Hare's child woke him from his nap.

"Daddy! Daddy! Daddy, somebody. Wake up, Baba! Somebody's coming, Daddy!"

Mr. Hare, opening his eyes slowly, asked, "What is the matter again, my son?"

"Police!"

"Po—what?"

"Police, Daddy!"

"Police?"

"No, wildcats!"

"Wild what?"

"Panther."

"Son, go to sleep. You are feeling sleepy!"

"Sleep and wait for the panther, Daddy."

"Liar!"

There was a knock at the door. Mr. Hare sat up instantly. His eyes swelled with surprise. Four men dressed in masks stood outside. The knocking resumed. He tiptoed to the small opening in the wall and saw two men whom he could not recognize with much ease. He seemed to recognize one of them, but he could not be sure. He ran back to his son and told him not to show or tell the men his whereabouts.

The place was dark and stinky. Some dead rotten rat was in the granary where the Hare hid himself from the men who were calling him from the other side the house. "Son, don't tell them that I am in the barn here. Have you got me? Don't tell them that I am in the granary."

There was a harder knock on the door. The men—those animal police—pushed the door off its hinges. The door came out of its position and fell onto the floor.

Guns, clubs, and spears were in the men's hands.
"Little dog," one of them said, "where is your master?"
The son of Hare just glared at the men blankly in silence.

"Little fool, where is your father?"

"Father?"

"Yes, your father!"

He looked at the granary and looked at the men in their eyes.

"Father? No, I don't know. I am an orphan."

"Orphan? Orphan, where is your father?"

"Father? Yes, Father is not there. I will not tell you that Father is hiding …"

He looked at the granary again and looked at the men. His father's teeth shattered against one another with fear.

"You see, son, the king wants to give your father the biggest gift of all time for performing a heroic action in building the well," explained one of the army police.

"Oh! That one? Don't waste your time now. If he comes back, I will tell him."

"Little Hare, you don't know how privileged the king would be if you could tell me your father's whereabouts now, you see?" urged another armed policeman.

"What has my father stolen from you that you come for him with clubs, guns, and spears?"

"Nothing, little 'un!" We told you why we need to see your daddy, didn't we?"

"Of course you didn't, but I will not tell you that Daddy is … hiding … in … the … gra-na-ry, you cops. I won't!" said the Little Hare.

"Surely?"

They rushed to check the granary on the compound. Thinking that the police were coming for him, Mr. Hare leaped out like a tree frog that could jump from England to Africa. Running got them all. The distance Mr. Hare left for the cops was alarming.

"Daddy, dodge them. Daddy, dodge them among the bananas. Daddy, leap higher. Oh, Daddy has dodged! Ha-ha-ha. Look, police. The … worn-out bottom … the … chick … clucked—*kwiok* has fallen! Ha-ha." Little Hare laughed louder and louder as his father successfully dodged the cops and finally escaped from them smartly.

*

In the second meeting held without Mr. Hare without apology, the Lion spoke very bitterly about the kind of men who were retarding the development programs in the Republican Jungle. He passed bylaws that would ensure order all times. He was annoyed with some, such as Mr. Hare, who had always dodged communal works and gotten away with it. He amended the constitution and replaced some of the old laws in the jungle that all animals were to abide by come rain or shine. The major jungle rules or laws put forward were as follows:

1. A king is born a king and dies a king.
2. The first and the last man is the king.
3. Treason is punishable by guillotine or by feeding snakes with the criminal.
4. Punishment for other crimes is one hundred years of banishment.
5. No work and no water for a convicted criminal.
6. Twenty strokes, an Oxfam of alcohol, and a fine of ten thousand shillings for he or she who is found guilty of a crime.

Mr. Hare had violated of the article, so he was liable to the prescribed medicine of twenty cups of pain, and his family to do some local chemistry for an Oxfam of alcohol, or else he would face death.
The game of Mr. Hare happened not only once but many times. His ax was still strong. The God of his mother was still strong. One day, his ax would fall in water.

The digging of the well took three solid days, both day and night. The female animals cooked and brought food for their men at the workplace. Any male animal whose wife did not bring food for the communal workers would be fined to brew a twenty-liter jerrican of Kwete, a local fermented alcoholic drink that took time to get the drinker drunk. The effect of it on the drinker was not worse than that of beer.

Having dug the well, the animals fenced it up with strong pegs and hooked thorns from the reach of thieves and their children who tended to play with the water. But after just one day, it was reported that a thief had started stealing water from the well. This made the king call for another meeting, in which they decided on who would keep the water source safe. Names were suggested, but no one would accept the position as guard of the water source without being paid wages or a salary. They said all work deserves a reward. Besides, they feared to risk their lives since they did not know who the thief was who was doing such a hideous thing at their well.

After a fruitless struggle to get someone to sacrifice himself for the keeping of the well, Mr. Buffalo the Horny came up and declared his intention to help guard the water source. He boasted that he would horn the bastard to death if he caught him in his horn.

At the well, Mr. Buffalo lay down on his chest, his legs outstretched like the arms of an eagle. Yet he was barehanded, waiting patiently for whichever bastard so he could burst his stomach at once. He scratched his itching ears with a stick.

Out of the blue, he heard some funny sound coming from somewhere near the well. He stood and cocked his head to listen, trying to discern from which direction the footsteps were coming, but the strong winds took the sounds away immediately. He heard not only the thudding footsteps but also the chanting humming voice coming like a flying bumblebee. He stepped back and set his feet firmly on the ground to wait for the wiseguy. The nearer the footsteps came, the louder the voice was heard. When the voice got close to the well, it increased and sang as follows:

> I am the God of the Well,
> And here I come now.
> I am a blind god.
> I kill whomever I meet.
> I am a blind god.
> I kill whoever doesn't retreat.

The voice became louder and louder as it drew nearer and nearer. On hearing its deadly message, Buffalo the Horny turned on his heel and took off. And to this effect, Mr. Hare came out of a gourd, drew the water, and went back home without a single black spot on his skin—smiling all the way home and mocking the coward with some rare scatological satire. He reported this new mysterious being to the king, who called him cowardly names and promised him that he would not allow him to attempt to guard the well anymore, for there was nothing that chased animals from the well as Mr. Buffalo reported.

The second animal came up for the same mission. It was none other than Rhino the Piggy. Rhino had thick skin, extended lips, and thick legs. He was the only animal who did not know the importance of hair—or fur for that matter. His body was fully bald and wrinkled. Of all the animals there, he was the fattest. Many animals said he was fat from the animals' taxes like the pay-as-you-earn (PAYE) tax, the sin tax, and the vagrancy tax, among others.

Rhino went and lay on his chest, with his big legs stretched out forward and backward, waiting for the thief of water to come and see what the monkey had seen in the garden of peas. He swore upon his dead mother that he would split the culprit's head apart and skin the ghost alive. He was a heavyweight fighter. But where had he fought before?

Suddenly he heard the thunderous footsteps of the stranger coming. Still lying on the ground, he placed his head down slowly, like a dog waiting for a bone being picked clean by its master. The footsteps sounded terrifying. This made Rhino's stomach melt down considerably. The nearer the sound came, the more scared he became. He too, like his brave predecessor, the Buffalo, heard the song sung:

> I am the God of the Well,
> And here I come now.
> I am a blind god.
> I kill whomever I meet.
> I am a blind god.
> I kill whoever doesn't retreat.

This practice of sending someone to guard the water source scared everybody in the jungle. The Lion did not go himself but sent other animals to catch the thief or meet the God of the Well. Even though presents were promised to whomever would kill the thief, no one dared risk his life. All were cowards. Some said the reward of eating with the king for one week after killing the water thief was not worth their lives. The king thought twice and had this for the brave one:

KILL THE WATER THIEF. MARRY THE PRINCESS! read the message on the palace's entrance point. Many other animals read the message but shied away. Mr. Tortoise was heard asking for permission to be allowed to go and kill the thief or catch him alive, because either way was permitted. The animals shouted and said the ghost was too big for Tortoise. He should better keep silence if he loved his life. Nobody took him seriously. Nobody cared.

But on reading this sweet message, everybody cheered up Elephant the Heavyweight as he quaked with enthusiasm to kill the water thief and marry the king's beautiful daughter.
The Elephant signed his name in the Royal Book and promised to catch the thief, step on his stomach, and squeeze his intestines out. He went to the battlefield but lost it too. He ran away with heavy footsteps upon hearing the strange threatening voice and seeing the big round mysterious calabash rolling toward the water well.

A dead silence fell over the palace. Water was needed or else somebody would have to die that day. Seeing that no one could afford to catch the ghost at the well, the king finally allowed the Tortoise to try his luck, skills, and strength. If he died, he should blame nobody, said the king, because this was a battle of the strong, not of the weak.

Battles need more skills than strength, thought the Tortoise.

Mr. Tortoise first laid out his strategy and thought deeply before reaching the well. He knew he was going to meet a monster, the God of the Well, as many animals had been reporting about the song of the stranger.

Reaching the well, Mr. Tortoise settled himself down under a small bushy tree to wait for whatever was to come. He had already sacrificed his life, having agreed to die so that others could live when they had water to drink. He saw that each time this malevolent thief stole the water, the water levels fluctuated terribly.

Soon, he heard the stranger come—only a big brown round gourd rolling with nobody's help. The gourd rolled toward the water source. A heavy voice was blasting a song from it, the same song he had heard his predecessors relate after their narrow escapes from the well.

> I am the God of the Well,
> And here I come now.
> I am a blind god.
> I kill whomever I meet.
> I am a blind God.
> I kill whoever doesn't retreat.

The Tortoise hardened his heart into a solid stone. He waited patiently to splash the brain of the stranger with the walking stick held in his hand. His torn black coat covered some parts of his body.

"The God of the Well! Oh, I see. This is the moment I have been waiting for, for a long time, a moment when the mother hen picks the seeds but does not give them to her chicks. This is the moment to see who is who," he said in a low voice, audible to himself alone.

"Should I scream?" He continued, "If I scream, it will know where I am and come armed for an attack at me. Should I run like a rocket and hit the gourd of the god or the God of the Gourd? What if I miss the target? I shall be dead. If I run away, those cowards will say I am a coward full of impotent words. Should I call for help? Animals don't help others these days; they only help themselves. What if they don't come to my rescue? No. This is what I will do now. If I must face death, then death I shall face. A coward should return to his mother's womb. A male tortoise will be seen in fire." This long soliloquy gave courage to the Tortoise, who, after gaining enough courage, waited for the rolling gourd to reach him so that he could hit it and break it into pieces. He decided to kill or to be killed. "A male tortoise is seen in fire!" he repeated loudly. But the noise the rolling gourd was making made the stranger in the gourd not able to hear the swearing of the Tortoise. Ready like nothing was the Tortoise. The singing. The rolling. The gourd. The God of the Well finally drew to the teeth of the wiser, with a heavy club in his hands held up high, waiting.

"Mother, come out, and I'll replace you in your grave!" He swore at once. Bwah! The gourd came into two pieces, and out of the water gourd the shameless thief shot himself, running for his home as if he had springs on the soles of his feet. You needed to be there to see how he ran for his life. He could not help laughing at the outsider. The God of the Well sprang for his life. The strong got the strength; the weaklings got the skills. But skills are stronger than strengths. The *gomasi* of goatskin was spread inside out. The winds blew, and the buttock of a chicken was ripped open.

The story of the courageous Tortoise was spread all over the jungle. No animals, huge as they might be, would dare say any disdainful words or call Mr. Tortoise queer names. Since that time, His Excellency the Lion paid homage to his son-in-law more than seldom.

SOME RISE, SOME FALL

Some rise by false methods; some by false methods do fall:
The devil's sooner praised and raised
Than the damn'd; truth is rewarded by righteous evil,
O immortal earth! What a blameworthy praise!
Gone are the days when the truth wins;
Things have chang'd, and so have the days.
Life is born when it's already very much torn.
Like cirrus clouds caught high in a daze,
Lie to be loved; tell the truth to be hated.
O righteous world! What a sacred sin!
Take my whole love, though belated,
As the sun sets in the east just therein.
Counting the rigged days, counting the hours,
The virgin hourglass broke her beauteous pow'rs.

HORNS OF THE UNICORNS

Remind me of my name,
Master;
Whisper to me my real name,
Dear sir,
Lost in the ashes of the game,
But forever.
Metallic rubbers rub lives off,
Born to die;
I am an eyewitness without an eye,
Both gouged out.
After the celebration drumbeats,
Throbbing like a panting heart,
Sounding like clan drum,
Was your sharp name
In the funeral of enemies.

Who am I, the civilian
Who is called your soldier?
Who am I if not yet a full fool?
I suffer from forgetfulness.
Oh, what have I just said?
You see? I have forgotten now.
What is my forgotten name?
What's my name? Let me know.

The one I used on the voter's card
When I thumbed up the blue print,
Signing my own death certificate.
I suffer from sch ... sch ... sch ... help me!
How do you call my sickness?
I suffer from forgetfulness.
Oh, what have I just said?
You see? I have forgotten now;
Sch ... sch ... schizophrenia.
Oh, that's it! You see how foolish I am?
I like forgetting at once
And repeating my old mistakes
Of not recognizing who you are,
Because I have the head of a chicken.

I have now forgotten all things,
Those you promised
While licking the tongue of spear,
Those that you would do for this community.
I have forgotten walking
Through the valley of the shadow
Of death you manufactured for me,
Risking my snake-shadow life,
Enduring the insults hurled
At the private parts of my mother
As I lifted you upon the ladder,
Hoping for your help someday
From your wet golden palms,
When mountains of tuition
Fall on my hunchback,
Nurturing my kwashiorkored children
As I spend my last dime on them.

I wonder why I keep believing

That someday you will clear
The mountains and elephants
From my sore head and shoulders,
Yet you have shown
False dawns in more ways
Than one—
All you care about is the dollars
And your family, friends, and in-laws.
Well done, Mr. Horrible Sir.
Your accountability is transparent
Like the wings of white ants.
But I lost the addiction to hope
In your courtships.

"No change, puppet master!" I sang,
Eyeing your bread and wine,
The real body and blood of Christ.
But ha-ha-ha-ha—you know what?
You are damn funny,
Mr. Horrible Sir.
Your mouth is bigger than your head,
Your head is bigger than your heart,
And your heart is like the head of a squirrel.
Blind heart! Dumb heart! Lame heart!
Your heart suffers from your industrial lies;
Both of you have a conjoined heart,
Like twins whose hearts are married.
The blood of lies is in you,
Conquering your blocked arteries.
Anyone who fools with you dies young.
Death is poisonous,
And poison is deadly.
I witnessed your crooked ways;
They are straight highways to hell.

Some die in peace, some in wars,
Some in pieces, some wholesomely,
Some at schools, some in bars,
Some in hospitals, some at home,
Some in the bush, some in bathrooms,
Some in classical aerodynamic fashion,
Some on altars, some in bedrooms,
Some in silence, some in a rootless dynamic.
Some die flat without falling sick,
Some without beholding their grandchildren,
Some without holding a walking stick.
Some die without tasting their chicken.
Whichever formula they forcibly take to die,
None is allowed to speak the truth but must lie.

Thus,
Whose horns do you wear, immortal man,
O human beast or beastly human?
You have the horns of the unicorns,
With purple and scarlet horns,
With angelic garments,
With a devilish heart.
Your harmless horns harm only the underprivileged:
The doctors, the teachers,
The sick, the jobless,
The orphans, the innocent,
The poor, the truthful,
The righteous, the widows,
The oppressed, the ignorant,
The needy, the child soldiers,
The mourners, the fooled,
The handsome-hearted, the beautiful-hearted,
While your enormous wings
Provide free safe haven for assassins,

For the country cowards,
For the mafia, for the ungodly,
For the sneerers, for the arrow boys,
For the law keepers who are the lawbreakers,
For the devil's disciples,
Soon to be crucified on the cross.

O my virgin father of lies,
I like how you amuse the masses,
Undressing your pair of buttocks,
For the masses to see and cry.
The more lies you tell,
The longer your tail grows,
And your horns surpass ordinary lives.
You praise thugs
And award them medals
For jobs well performed
In enlarging the country's cemetery,
Increasing the salaries of coffin makers,
For they do not rest.

The lies you conceive
Impregnate you,
And you give birth to flies,
For you are the Lord of the Flies.

Pass again and bang my head
Against your crown of blood,
As you have always done,
Till the good Lord saves the nations.

I cannot conquer my thoughts
Clouded in my dumb mind,
Eyeing your sacks of dimes,

Anointing my feet and palms,
Bread and wine,
Your bread and wine,
Are the true body and blood of Christ,
Respectively.

I do not repent of my past mistakes,
Of following you without goggles,
Eating with you without a fork.
I have that organic stubbornness
Of following a snake that bit me
For thirty years and so on.

My appetite for you, Daddy,
Is like the appetite for a newly wedded bride,
Sooner drunk, sooner fooled.
One fool fools many …

You immortal being
With the beauty of a gorilla,
With birds of the same feather
Flocking around you like feces flies,
Flapping wings and tapping tears,
Like a dragon bat tapping Nigerian palm wine.

Mr. Horrible Sir,
Well done. You taught me
That I must eat with a long fork
While eating with death;
That I must carry my own cross
And follow you with cowardice;
That—
"Serve yourself or starve to death.
Help yourself or die alive alone.
Rise up and bury your own dead!"

THE KNOTTED HEART

Some by lots, some ballots, O usurpations!
Yet neither Caesar nor thou standeth lot;
But precedence for the next generations,
Thine set in bellyaching heart of the knot,
The future decided by men who dig graves,
To be hungry free men or well-fed slaves.

O this vile usurper! Thou inglorious glory.
O dishonorable rank! Inglorious rank of sins,
Nights weary and dreary and wry and teary.
Inglorious monarch! Tears in brimful basins,
Inglorious divinity! O red iron hand.
Red levins rumble as if drunk, old band!

Dream voters! Future bleak! Dream voters,
Heavens groan in the hands of predators!

MAMMON

O this damned beauteous beloved evil
Whichfor thou search'st me to slay,
Or thou art stalk'd by stance to be killed
Every passing spoilt night and sad day!
O this buttressed rooted evil doth show
With its main roots in ranks of scavengers,
And now their bloody teeth they do draw
For thirty shekels, red blades of avengers.
Stately they climb ladders against tearful rain,
For which sacrificial dead souls sold,
And they clenched their teeth, enduring the pain
Of sweet rod, God-given charms, and gold.
Thou sayest, "No glove, no love."
Thy intents of her I disapprove.

WEAVERBIRDS

Two types of weaverbirds
Rock this eucalyptus tree,
The black and the yellow ones,
Both larger than Thailand.
White elephants, seriously.

Their barracks hang down
Like testicles of beasts,
Woven like baskets along riversides,
On this groaning tree and maize garden;
They chant. These canonized birds sing.

Deep scars are left on the cobs
From their clawy ironed beaks
Peeling the teeth of the maize,
Leaving them toothless like cops.
What will we the poor peasants eat?

These birds have an irresistible appetite
For preaching the good tidings
Of hunger in our motherland
Come the month of touching
Women's pretty, gnawing faces.

These holy birds, Republican birds,
Dress in yellow from pants to hats
As they mate in the garden of maize,
Planting hunger in the fatherland.
They preach of their second coming.

THE HAIR OF THE MONSTER

The hair of the ogre had become a great burden to him. So one day, he roasted some very nice-tasting and good-smelling groundnuts to look for someone who could help him shave off his long and bushy forest of hair. Many animals refused to help him because they knew him as a cannibal. No one would fall into Mr. Monster's hands and escape, giving him the day's meal. Many lives had been claimed by this heartless monster who had no mercy, not even a drop of it, because not even the elephants could match his enormous strength. All the animals feared the monster. Anyone who dared compete with him would be his supper. He was feared near and beyond the seven ridges of Montana.

After a long and tiresome seeking for a person who would agree to shave off his long and bushy hair hanging down his head like stalactites, as if by magic he came across Mr. Hare, who was digging in his farm, whistling and humming a song for which there were no words. This hare thought so deeply and suddenly jumped up. He had gotten an idea. As soon as Mr. Monster told him of his great ordeal of his long and painful search for a helper, the hare agreed after negotiating the terms and conditions applied. He knew what it took to brush a lion's teeth with a short toothbrush. His life could be at a stake. He knew why other animals feared the monster like death. He knew every bit of what there was to know about him. He knew this in the back of his mind—but the agreement was only reached after a deep, long, and hard third thought.

"A game we shall play! The mother bird feeds the nestling!" said the monster.

"Ha-ha! Yes, sir. You really know how to play chess! And Omweso too? I mean the game is called 'play with my belly, but not my mind.' I know how much you love games. Which number do you play, master?" responded the Hare, his voice rather sarcastic in tone.

"I played that game when I was younger than a baby—when I was in my mother's womb. It was called a waiting game."

"No longer shall it be called so. It will be called a crying game!"

"Your tears are many, I suppose. No wonder. But all I need is one. Help me do the work—a simple work. As simple as writing one."

"Easier said than done! Just give me the work. Twenty-one years on the streets—jobless!"

"You look desperate."

"A hungry man doesn't know a bitter-tasting sauce. Everything is sweet to him. Swear you won't deceive me."

"Warts and all. In fact, a princely reward awaits you, I swear!" He humbled himself, his eyes gleaming with pleasure that the victory was already his.

"A work is better with a reward. I know that. No say."

"Your speed saves your life. The faster, the safer and the better!" This statement that the monster made was not well heard because he had a heavy voice, so the hare didn't much value what he vaguely heard.
The hare demanded that Mr. Monster first give him the groundnuts before he placed his fingers on his, the monster's, head. Because he

was faster than a machine, he was no amateur at barbering heads. *Otwong wille ki otwong*—which literally means "one good turn deserves another."

When given the groundnuts full of delicacy, the hare first drank them up like water and placed the groundnut bag on the ground. Then, slowly but surely, he started cutting the monster's head of hair with a broken glass—because he could not afford to buy a razor blade. He had hardly finished shaving off one part of the head when he suddenly saw the grasses of hair grow up like the magic bean that grew and touched the sky.

"Wonders will never cease! What a mystery!" exclaimed the hare, more amazed than annoyed.
He wanted to tell the monster about what he saw, but he deemed it wiser to keep silent. Then he murmured something to himself.

The monster did not hear a thing. He was busy removing wax from his large ears. The wax was like sewage waste stuck in the pathway in the pipeline. The smell of the wax attracted a bee to the stick in his hand. You never could imagine the speed with which the monster stood, in anger and pain, his threatening finger pointing at Mr. Hare.

"You told me you could do the work. Is that what you could do to me, Job? Is that what you could do?"

"What is it now? Has it come to that yet? I don't know …"

"What don't you know? What don't you know, eh?"

"Please, I don't want trouble. I am just a barber."

The ogre, knowing that the hare had done nothing wrong, sat down and commanded him to finish his head quickly.

As the hare finished the other side of the head, he saw that the part he had shaved off had grown up again. He felt bitter and disappointed, wondering why he had accepted the task in the first place.

At this point, he devised a mean. He told the ogre that the ogre had a great deal of lice on his head that needed picking away. As he climbed and started pretending he was picking the lice away, the niceness of the soft touch of Mr. Hare made the monster fall asleep.

Seeing that the monster was slowly falling asleep, the hare waved his hand carefully in front of his face to check the depth of his sleep. Then he gathered enough energy and jumped down like an orangutan on a tree branch. No sign of consciousness was shown by the monster. Slowly, but certainty, the hare slipped off like a fish from a fishnet. He had not fully escaped when the monster woke up, screaming after him.

"Oh no! Oh no! You are gone, you charlatan bastard! You eat my groundnuts and run away? You are gone now. You are finished, Hare! If death wants to kill you, your body itches. You will vomit my groundnuts all—all!"

He got up onto his feet and began chasing after Hare with a terrible speech, but he was too heavy to run very fast. Hare ran so fast that he left in his wake a memorable distance for Mr. Monster to ravel. He sped toward Mr. Tortoise's home down the valley. Montana is full of grave hills and valleys.

"Help! Help! Tortoise, help! The ugly Satan wants to kill me! Help!" screamed Mr. Hare, rather tired now.

On hearing the alarm, Mr. Tortoise, who by then was eating in his house with his wife and three children, was startled by the noise. He came out to rescue the hare as the latter was about to be caught and torn to pieces.

As the tortoise asked where the troublemaker was, he ran for his walking stick under the door and then ran out to meet the monstrous monster.

Mr. Hare jumped like a flea behind his new benefactor and peeped from his Tortoise's shoulders. How the tortoise and the monster clashed with words, which mounted into real quarrel. In the fight that ensued, the tragic moment drew nearer as Mr. Tortoise pushed the ogre back with the stick. His last-born child, named Breakspeare, ran to stop the fight, but as his father swung the stick overhead and then behind him, the stick struck Breakspeare on the head and he dropped dead.

Furiously, as he saw his son lying on his ear in a pool of blood, the tortoise rushed toward Mr. Monster, with eyes as large with anger as Chinese balls, and hit him in the head three times till he lay on the ground helplessly, blood gushing from his head and ears and mouth as he bled profusely. Then he took his last breath.

"Death is no respecter of a monster," remarked Hare as he rushed into the house of Mr. Tortoise for the royal drum. "Nothing too small is too weak and useless, and nothing too big is too useful and strong. All that treads can be treaded on," added he while picking up the stick and tying the drum around his waist. He started singing and drumming and dancing. The song he sang went as follows:

> The monster's species disappear.
> The animals' species reappear.
> The monster's species disappear.
> The animals' species reappear.
>
> What is better than humans?
> The monster's species disappear.
> The animals' species reappear.
> What is better than humans?

This explains why the animal species exist but monsters are extinct.

THE UNINVITED GUEST

It spoke in tongues,
Metallic tongues of book.
It came like a thief at night,
Like a fire without smoke.
Through flawless blood,
In a military coup,
It stayed among us here.
It came among us here.
We welcomed it hospitably,
With bread and sweet wine,
Traditional dances and mock fights.
It said it fought for our rights,
But in fact
It fought for its own rights,
To abuse our rights.
Never did we know it.

It said it was our real brother,
With skin as black as mine
(Since we gave it that wine),
But unfortunately
It had a long nose
That you call a trunk,
That I call ivory.
Out I was flung!
It flung me out of my house.
With its nose taller than itself,
It stayed in my house
And altered the rule of my house
That welcomingly says,
"Good guests know when to leave!"
Changing it to its own rule
That resistantly says,
"Good guests never leave unless by fire!"
So it became our master,
And we became its servants.
It touched the book of laws,
And crowned itself lifelong king
Of the republican jungle.

It introduced numerous rules
Governing the usage of our ancestral land
And indicating how we must pay our sin taxes.
It detained its opponents
And assassinated others,
And advised its advisors.
It mated day and night
And reproduced like white ants,
Feeding its offspring on my cassava.
It had a hat bigger than a winnowing pan
And a heart as blind as a bat.
It thanked me for milking my cows with ease,
Which became its own cows.
By matter of death and life,
My royal stool became its footstool,
And my servants its slaves.
I was once a king in my house,
But now I am a slave king
Of the black elephant,
The uninvited guest.
Since the white elephant left,
I have never known what you call freedom …

UPPER ROOM

In the upper room,
I led her to rest,
And her baby for dollars,
In the red dark room,
Pounded yams of head,
Pounded in the mother mortar,
For the dollars on altar;
No peace, no sleep.

I am dead alive,
Rotten from the inside.
The pain they cry
On the outside,
I cry on the inside.
Drumbeats of pains
Boom in my veins.
Talking drums of pains,
Surely, I suppose.
The devil gives to you
To take you.
By the left hand given;
By the right hand taken.
No peace, no sleep.

In the upper room,
Where they speak in tongues,
Infernos baptize me,
Raging in my heart
Like a rapture of bonfire.
And my breath is bitter,
My soul torn apart,
As I give them to be given,
My wishes, my burdens.
Down the dust leading me,
Slowly in pangs.
Death is slow when pain is much.
Slowly in pangs,
Death is slow if you want to leave fast.

In the upper room,
Down at the bottom of darkness,
My wife and baby groan.
My house stands on blood,
Bathing my highway to the grave.
Monsters laugh
Beneath my golden bed.
My wish to live like billionaires
Taking me down the narrow house,
Seven feet deep down.

In the upper room,
Cankers are hungry,
Feeding on my skins,
Falling off like spent bullets;
My resilient improvement
Escorts me home,
Down the dark tunnel,
A dance to infernos;
White ants of flying dollars
Watch me happily as I leave sadly,
My dreamy wish to the flesh of dust:
Better to die poor but happily
Than to live rich but unhappily.
Be careful what you wish for.

MORTAL DANCE

Upon old baobabs,
high upon heathen heavens,
rattles of gods roared,

stretching their spears
high to the roof of the heavens,
piercing the ribs of angels,

and letting out the blood
of angels to appease the gods
of the sinful earth.

The heathen herdsmen
roar back to the bleeding heavens
in protest of mortal impulses,

fighting back for life,
uproaring for the act of herem,
their hearts colder than ice.

Echoes of the mourning clouds
rumbled across the red skies
with detached heads full of hell

in the dance of the civilized savage,
in their happy mortal dance.

ODE TO A FALLEN SOLDIER

Okot, son of Bitek,
Son of my mother,
Son of the soil,
I will well keep your words
As your name that sounds like a clan drum.
Our people say that
Waters of a relative are poured behind him,
So here I pour my waters behind you,
Waters full of life.
Your words still fall in my ears
Like spent bullets in the game of Russian roulette,
Reloading your used gun for my use,
Not to rust like an overdue emotion.
Though your body is nowhere to be found,
I know you hear me from your narrow house;
Your body may rot, but not your words.

Lawino still sings her songs
That Africa hears around fireplaces.
She stills sings of her mean husband.
She still sings of her husband whose head sleeps outside.
She still complains of her husband
Whose head has been twisted by Clementina.
Lawino is sulky.

She is sulky because her husband no longer loves her.
His love for her has been tottered by Clementina.
Clementina has taken over her home.
Lawino still sings of her castrated bull
Whose testicles have been smashed by big books,
Those forests of books from Makerere University,
Scattered all over the house like a house of a teacher,
Cladded with iron sheets of papers.

My blood brother,
Lawino still sings of Africa in the rubbish pit;
She still sings of her pearl of Africa.
Her words are used up;
I am the only word left in her mouth,
The last bullet in the gun,
But your boots are too big for my wearing.
I am planning to take over Lawino from Ocol,
Whose head now sleeps outside.

Son of my mother,
Your expired memory keeps my memory fresh
Like fresh milk put in a fridge,
The memory of you remains fresh like a chalk line at a crime scene.
Your "Song of Malaya" and "Song of a Prisoner"
Are like lightning when the clouds are pregnant.
They strike dry fig trees and wet tamarind,
Where weaverbirds sound their jingle bells,
Building their skyscraper nests with our hands.

Son of Gulu Town,
No longer do I see your twinkling insightful eyes

Or your body entwined with mine
Like the roots of adjacent giant Kituba trees
That have shared storms in the dark;
No longer do your eloquent lips,
Seasoned with Acholi salts,
Whisper poetry and folktales to my hollow, ailing ears.
You left a cold chasm
Where you once sat,
Teased folks with witty ridicule
Seasoned with Acholi wisdom.
Your head had blown enough air,
And your tongue eaten enough Acholi salts.
Your songs were baskets of honey
That everyone wished to taste
As they pealed rippling laughter.
But now you lie hidden from my eyes
Like a black palm fruit hidden in a dust of ash.

Each time I sip on your perfumed words,
They keep me awake like the perfume of a bride
Who has just left for her father's house,
Never to return.

Your words of wisdom
Still linger around fireplaces
Like lost spirits that have got no place in the rivers or big trees
When chased away from heaven as rebel souls,
So they still have a long way to go
As long as Africa sleeps in the rubbish pit
Or defecates by the roadside.
Some words fall on infertile ears,
Some on rocky grounds,
Some on fertile hearts.
I used to hope that you would come back someday,

But I have lost my addiction to those hopes now,
Except in those words that pierce the hearts of men
With humor and wisdom.

Though you wasted no time in leaving me,
I have used up my ears for crying for you.
Instead I am unable to cry,
Except for the fact that the old dog is still running.
Our people say that old dogs don't run for long,
But this one has passed the test of time;
It has metallic hands and a metallic chest for running.
It is still shepherding the flock with rods,
If you can see it from your narrow house.

Okot, son of Bitek,
The breed of elephants,
This horn of love has pierced my heart.
I have got your hidden treasure,
The hidden pot of ink and quill,
But before I write a poem for your kinsmen
And the regime you left in power,
Let me first go and have my luncheon.
The regime has prepared a cow for breakfast
And a beast for lunch.

ONE BRIDE, TWO HUSBANDS

Suddenly came the question that sent shivers running down my spine. I had been waiting for this time to come from wherever it was in the hideout—possibly in the vestry. I had very much expected this, but with little surety of the answer. Though all along I knew it would always be as others had always said it would be when they came to this revered place. Finally, it came as I saw Reverend Jude standing up and smiling at us. I showed him a little grin too, and then I flashed a bigger one at my wife, who by this time could not help smiling back. He cleared his throat once again, as if with an intention for something, then popped out the question from his nicely shaped holy lips as he drew near us on the altar: "I bless you both, beautiful young souls, in union," murmured he softly.

The laymen, best men, best women, flower girls and boys, and all the others stood side by side next to us, waiting faithfully and delightfully. And a bevy of beauties on the front pews, dressed in snow-white attire, welcomed the newcomers, both the invited and the uninvited guests, both the guests of honor and the guests of horror, to the party in the church.

After a few murmurs, Reverend Jude cleared his throat once again. It seemed he'd eaten a lot of fat the night before that kept blocking the air from his lungs. "Ladies and gentlemen," began he, the echoes reverberating like the voice of a ghost in a dark cave. "A moment of silence! Is there any reason as to why these two should not become husband and wife?" asked the reverend.

All the happy noises were suddenly suppressed and swallowed up by the hungry silence. Not even a soul dared whisper. Each person in the congregation kept looking behind for who would shoot himself or herself first to reject the union of the two in love, as if it was a must for the betrayer to come from behind. One by one, everybody started looking at us once again. Thousands of eyes daringly, enthusiastically, and expectantly glared madly at me and her. I bit my lower lip as Lydia's milk-white eyes glowed like two stars in the night. But for her case, her eyes kept on swelling with brave fears as my heart panted with a sick speed. *Who will say what, why, and about whom?* That was now the only worrying question lingering in my mind.

Somebody suddenly coughed intentionally, and all eyes went in his direction, expectantly. I stood high on my toes to see who it was. The joker was not visible as the congregation was like a flood of water.

I recollected myself and held Lydia's hands in my hands; we collectively smiled at each other. Her warm smile was contagious like the Black Death that once walked through Europe. I kept looking directly into her eyes, her body inside the white spiderwebbed wedding gown that swallowed her up like a hungry python. She and I were dressed to kill and were, thus, so damn smart that a housefly feared to cross near us. A hyena would cross our path from afar. I was dressed in my borrowed black suit. The cameramen kept flashing their inconvenient camera lights.

I felt a cold drop on the Afro hair on my head. Touching my head to find out what it was, I picked off a bird's dropping. Looking up over my head, I saw a cooing dove kissing a crow. One cameraman was sharp enough to see the birds and shoot their photos at once. A dozen people, I suppose, saw what I saw too. My wife-to-be's eyes still gleamed as she simultaneously kept looking at the gathering and me. I resolved myself once again. I wondered why Reverend Jude was wasting time waiting for an answer that was not there. He repeated the same question. A similar reaction was given as a response. Inside the white spiderwebbed wedding gown was my bride-to-be, sweet Lydia. All had attended this white wedding.

Fleets of luxuriant cars I had never seen before (but of course, I had seen them in Hollywood movies) could be seen outside, lining up with their sides and their rears facing the churchyard.

Five similar red presidential cars roared outside. It would be a great pleasure to have the president or his disciples attend my wedding ceremony. The president always poured a mournful amount of money into any wedding ceremony as this, or better yet into the funerals of opposition leaders. A particular pleasure for this peculiar arrival overwhelmed me. Few took notice, though. All eyes were on us. My anger was slowly overtaking me now. Why would the reverend ever take this much wasteful time?

Suddenly, my heart cooled down as I saw the reverend move toward us. His eyes showed a definite assurance. *What is yours remains yours even if you refuse it, and what is not yours can never be yours even if you force it,* I thought to myself. He had hardly tilted the microphone when five men, one of them dressed in all red—dark red goggles, red bow tie, red suit, and red shoes, with a pointed face—and the other four dressed in all black, came in, slowly passing by the congregation on their way to the altar. Two gunmen remained guarding the giant exit door, which similarly acted as the entry point for all. The two men who escorted the man in all red signaled to the escorts, or rather bodyguards, to stand aside and leave him to talk alone. The two faithful men obeyed the order as raging fears caught the masses.

"I do," said the man in red. The reverend's trousers danced fretfully. His eyes grew wide with surprise, and he paused to breathe for a second or so.

The man pointed at me. "You, David, you will not get away with your hideously dark act. You must pay the price." I looked at myself, doubting if I was the one being talked to. I had to look behind me and then sideways to make sure that I was the one being talked to.

"You, Lydia," said the stranger, pointing at my bride, "you *betrayed* me! And for that reason you will never see your beloved David again. He's already dead."

I felt like I'd gotten an electric shock that shook me up and that dried up all my blood and all speech from my mouth. *What have I done?* I asked myself, still living in doubts. As the men did an about-face, my spirit started coming back to my flesh, slowly. The congregation, full of fear, looked at one another agape. "What the hell is going on?" they asked themselves rhetorically. As the man in all red stepped out of the cathedral, my wife fell down, blood trickling from her rib. Had a silencer been used? A revolver could have reported to me the perpetrator. I looked at the men as they were leaving, quaking with anger. I looked at my bride down near my feet with lots of pity—not knowing whether to chase the men or bend down to collect my fallen wife. As the men sped away with clouds of dust covering their red cars, and as the congregation dropped down on their feet and made for the narrow exit, I bent down finally to collect my bleeding bride. The reverend had already disappeared like a naked knife.

All of St. Peter's Cathedral remained for me and my wife, whom I carried out against my bloodied chest to wait for any passing vehicle to give us a lift to the nearest hospital. Tears kept on ejaculating from my red eyes in mournful numbers. My chest was wet with the blood and the tears. The door to the cathedral remained open. The statues of Mary and Jesus welcomed us both. The blood in the cathedral remained wet and scarlet. We still stood by.

THE PROMISED RAPE

The soothsayer prophesied
Your several comings to love me.
All your love tricks in the book,
Now I know like a fool
Knows the back of his own hand:
Your divide-and-rule love policy;
Your opportunistic friends and in-laws love policy;
Your cat's paw assassin love policy.
All my family has known.
Every night of Christmas Eve,
You bring me a bar of salt
And a packet of soap;
A poor man has no choice.
This Hobson's choice works.
You promise me heaven on earth
And then love till the reaper parts us.
This night is the promised night—
You lie in the name of God.
After intercoursing my virginity,
You run about in celebration
Of your scored goal—splinter in my womb.
You have achieved your mission,
Your hundreds visions of division.
My name is no more in your brain;

I smoke the dust of your cars.
The elevator drives you up and down.
I am just the branch of the tree
You used as a ladder to climb,
Your tree of progress to hell.
Now that you have beaten my fire,
Only ashes are left for me to taste;
I can't see you for the dust of your cars.

COSMETOLOGY

Welcome, my beautiful class;
Today we're gonna look at a new topic
Called cosmetology.
If I may ask,
What is cosmetology?

Me, sir—study of cosmoses.

No, not correct.
That is cosmology.

Sir, it is the study of the white man's
Coming to colonize Africa.

No, that's damn wrong.

Hmm. Me, sir—it's the study of the squalor
And poverty of the African cities' slums,
Their corrupt and despotic leaders,
And soil erosion of African cultures.

No, Suubi. Listen now, class:
This is the study of the cosmetic industry
And its effect on your mothers and sisters.

What are some of the cosmetic products your mothers
And beautiful sisters use always?

Sir, me—ashes!

Ashes? Oh, no! Think deeper again, Kaka.

Me, sir—curry powder!

Oh, that's wrong, dear Phiphi.

Hmm—skin burner, sir.

Yes, you're quite right, Nancy.
Class, give Nancy thunderous handclaps.
(Handclaps.)

Very good!
As heavy a handclap as an angry thunder.

Now, in Senior I,
We learned of a few examples of cosmetics,
But this time around,
We shall look at them all today.
The first one is emery boards, nail clippers, ambis.

No, you're wrong, sir.

Suubi, we have nothing like wrong answers.
All answers are correct,
But some questions are wrong—
For the given correct answers.

Then me, sir—the devil's fingernails

And a dead white man's hair.
(The class laughs.)

Foundation,
Concealer,
Blusher,
Powder,
Eyeliner,
Eye shadow,
Lip gloss,
Lip liner,
Lipstick.

Those are the types of makeup my sisters use, sir.

And lip metal, sir.

No lip metal,
But mascara.

And lips of a lion licking its kill's blood, master.

Don't call me "master," Suubi.
I am not a slave driver.
(The class laughs wholesomely.)

What is makeup used for, class?

Me, sir—to close heaven and open hell.

No, sir, Toldo is wrong. Me, sir—to whiten the blackness of an African woman.
A white woman in black skin …

Clap for brilliant Suubi, class!

It's a pleasure—a short clap (*Rrraaap!*)—the best girl.

Now listen—its hideous effect:
A black woman dies a white death.
That is the effect!

I have a question, sir.

Ask me, Suubi.

What do you mean, a black woman dies a white death?

I mean we have come to the end of the lesson.
Thank you. Have a good day.

Thank you, sir, for your service;
Your service is highly welcomed.
You, teacher, teach so well!

(The class sings.)

Thank you, teacher, for teaching us.
Everywhere we go,
People admire us.
We can't get tired because of you.

(The teacher leaves the room. The class laughs.)

I awake, relieved.
It was just a sweet dream.

Obella Stephen is a Ugandan poet, literature teacher, lyricist, and stage performer (strictly poetry). He was born in Teso Region, Amuria District, in February 1996. Obella Stephen is the founder of Teso Writers' Foundation (TWF) and a songwriter at Teso Young Blood Musical Empire (TYBE).

QUEEN OF THE ANTHILL

I madly beat these drums,
Louder than thunderous hell's bells,
As you hide deep down in the anthill
Between well-armed termites.
Mother of the anthill,
Mother of the white ants
Whose smiles are maize and who comb the spaces,
Pumping the heart of the moon.
Queen of the early morning sun,
Sing for me the sunbird songs
That made the hare dance until death,
That tore apart the frog's mouth
From one ear to the other ear.
I have folded my long tongue
And whistled your name to the jungle
To suffocate the bravest lion,
To impregnate virgin mosquitoes.
But I am lost in Nyero rock paintings,
Where early humans painted your picture,
Where white-faced witch doctors

Worship the goddess of the sea.
I am the Karamojong cattle raider
Who smelled the cow dung
Of your great-grandfather's cow
That you were grazing.
But you have raided my heart.
Shall we go to Pak-Owo clan, Asekenye,
Where wizards run faster than gun bullets,
Where night dancers jump to the cloud roof,
Where necklaces are made from river gold?

RAISE NO WEAPONS

Raise no more weapons, nor glittering swords,
For the poet's pen wilt rust 'em by liquid words.
Fold no fists; knock no man down,
For he who started war digs a grave of his own.
Divine's thy ink that preaches peace so fair.
Love, unite from toenail to thine last hair.
Let no big-bellied politician rape the book of law.
'Tis thee who fooled the masses to fall to graves below.
"No blood, no power; and no power without blood!"
Art echoes that melt like ice-made flood.
O let bright swords have no blood to spill,
Lest inkpots use't on sad scrolls and quill:
He who starts war pulls a poet's tail.
In historic pages doth he fail and fall, or fall and fail.
Let world peace, as candles, burn on and on,
For we desire a world with o'erwhelming hate gone.

THE WEEPING AFRICA

This is Africa,
Not the one you knew before,
Beautified in those colored maps,
But one lying on a deathbed,
Whose future is not in the future.
Come with me. Hold my hand
As I show you this land
Where political liars win the voters,
Yet those who speak the truth
Fall with legs facing upside down.
(Truth is political lies, and lies are political truth.)
This is Africa in reality,
Where politicians bribe skeletal voters
With poisonous alcohol
From Kill Me Quick breweries,
So they can vote when drunk,
Chanting mad slogans:
"Long live our dictator!"
"Give us more devil's tears, not food!"
Do drunk masses vote for good leaders?

This is a dying Africa,
Breathing on her deathbed
With eyes sunken in their sockets,

Like HIV/AIDS infection.
Those who overthrew corrupt leaders
By splashing blood by the sword
Became twice corrupt while in power.
Their elastic stomachs
Grew wider than larger water drums,
And their teeth became yellow egg yolk
With the poor man's taxes.

This is Africa,
Where justice is injustice
And injustice is justice.
"Let the criminals stay free.
As the innocent rot in jail!
Build more prisons, not schools!"
Our leaders chant,
But then, did they ever know
That an open school closes a prison,
That an open prison closes a school?

This is Africa,
Where frowning peace talkers
Hold pistols behind their backs.
Guns first, peace later.
No blood, no power.
Leaders must rule until they die,
Or even rule after death if they can.
(Yes, we can!).
Children are born in war and die in wars.
The supreme book of law
Must bow down to worship money.
No money, no justice.
This is Africa, my beautiful land.

DEATH CERTIFICATE

Pick up your red pen and a ballot paper
And sign the death certificate of my regime.
Or if you've never before seen a teacher's buttocks
In my who-cares-about-you-failing schools,
Then thumbprint my old face with your cracked hand.
Or else bullets shall open your empty head.
I am the ruler of life and death,
Emperor of the dead, the unborn, and the born.
There is no ballot power here in Africa.
Might is right; no war, no power.

See here, you stupid voter:
Vote for me and vote for life.
If you vote for another, then you vote for your death.
You are a mosquito between my thumbs.
I am the law, and the law is me,
The alpha and omega of this bloody nation,
I am the advisor of my advisors.

When I command, the gun releases bullets.
Bullets ask no question of my words.
So pick up your pen and the ballot paper.
Double-tick my old face again and again
So I may hold you in my political hands.
Listen if you have large, clean ears,
Or else you will be my gun's sweet meal.

BONY MASSES, FAT LEADERS

Rule fools, but lead the wise;
After all, hungry rats pounce on innocent mice.
Political gods widen their big bellies from our tax granary:
Eat our sweat, so we may only graduate in nursery.

No one is born a ruler, and no one rules after death:
Old man, cling to power till your final breath.

Build prisons and jail the innocent.
Only give justice to those who speak by cent.
On judgment day, you shall pay.
Kill by gun at night; pay by day.

Only the dead know the torments of grave worms.
Fight for power, but power will kill you.

Love your office more than the voters who put you into office.
Also kill by the sword; but by the sword thou shalt die.
Women you force to have sex with you shall too kill you.

SMOKE FROM THE GUNFIRE

"No blood, no power" is a political chant
Falling on innocent ears as the gun hunts.

Bullets carelessly leave the smoking gun;
Love for this nation ends where it began.
At gunpoint, breathe your last breath,
Or pray for life after forced death.
Dig your grave. Guns know no death time.

Never shall there be fire like the gunfire
Of lions ruling the jungles after they timely retire.

Power makes a good leader go blind,
Overruling the nation with his poorest mind.
We are not free outside rotting prisons,
Ever chained in frowning hearts.
Ruled by hungry metallic guns.

DOWN THE STREETS

Down these dusty streets,
The governmental guns splash blood in the air,
Blood of the red-eyed, folded-faced masses,
Bony, bare chests resisting the corruptible proboscis
That sucks taxes deep down pig-sized bellies.
Political gods singing rhythmical compositions
For God and my stomach's gluttonous lyrics.
"Arise, Arise! To arms, to arms!"
(He who comes to power by blood poured
Finds the taste of the sweet throne sour.)

Down these rotten streets
Move flocks of vultures, dogs, and buzzing flies,
Feasting on rotten dead bodies of freedom fighters
Who stormed these streets carrying change banners.
Street children weep over death graveyards.
False peace is preached by gunfire, not by tongues:
Silent lips, noisemaking guns.
(War kills peace, and peace kills war;
He who rules till old age rules not far.)

Down these flaming streets,
Street walls are painted by red blood.
My trembling hands turn on the radio
From the bush, where my poor life hides.
"The police no longer keep law and order;
They keep disorder and lawlessness.
One million burned inside the wagons;
The governmental gun says
All are guilty until proven innocent after death."
I turn off my radio and weep in silence.
"O beloved beautiful country!"
I cry. I cry, "Arise, arise!"

THE RAT ATE THE CAT

The stubborn rat grew long teeth
And ate the cat, swallowing it into its pregnant belly.
The tail led the empty head.
The brave fool led the wise man
To the kingdom of wisdom.
The world turned upside down.
The born are beautifully ugly
In the village of Osukut,
Where slaves rule their masters
And gods worship the worshippers:
The water swallowed bragging fire,
And hell ruled the heavens.
Ugly girls are the king's concubines,
As the beautiful are fuddy-duddy,
Women's breasts turned to their back.
The tiny David killed Goliath.
The world ran mad long ago.
Lizard feces wrote on the blackboards,
As men listened wide-eared.
Iculi's anus swallowed the hot sun.
The sword slayed the sword owner.

The frog remained in the vulture's throat,
Smiling from ear to ear.
The food choked the hungry man
As gluttons starved to death.
So, the cigarette smoked the smoker
And died of whooping cough.
The anus urinates, the penis defecates.
The stupid bird with a small anus
Swallowed a bigger seed.

BLOOD AND QUILL

I am a completely mad poet,
Thirsty for more blood in my inkpot,
Blood from a thousand weeping souls.
My hair is a forest of ideas,
Flowing in blood, which drip-drops down my quill,
Painting piles of scrolls and stone tablets,
Stretching from my table to the nimbus clouds,
From heaven to hell.
So I dream when awake,
And I am awake in my dream
As I hide inside this white linen.

I am not a bearded philosopher,
Nor am I the wise King Solomon,
For I am a man made of blood ink,
The king of my imaginary world,
Dipping my peacock quill in a pool of blood
As ideas pour down my burning scroll.
Bring more tablets to my table!
Lest my idea-made head burst open.

My round eyes are two burning globes.
I see the universe inside my tiny retinas.
I see hearts, minds, and souls
Inside my closed poetic eye:
So, give me that scroll, blood, and quill.
As a million words pass through my veins,
I shall build a heaven in hell,
Or a hell in heaven.
Set a candlelight in the dark.
Let me roll my quill on scrolls.

WHEN I AM GONE

I sit along the riverside,
Staring at slow-moving water.
This river is calm and peaceful.
As I weep tears downstream,
I keep asking myself painful questions:
Who shall remember my name?
When I am dead and gone,
Who shall sing my unsung songs
That were to heal the universe?
Who shall remember the words
That I wrote on the pages
Of many deserted souls?
No one shall remember this, I know;
So soon I shall fade,
Like every rose under the sun,
I shall wither and die.
Someday, I shall hold my breath
And take a long route to nowhere.
Many shall smile, I know,
With tears running down their masked faces.
This hurts me so much.
This torments my bleeding soul.
That is the reason I sit here,
By this rolling river,

Hoping to flow along its stream.
I would love to cry,
But I don't know how to start.
Teach me how to weep
So I shall weep for myself,
If no one else will do it for me.
But then I have to smile today.
I have made no history,
But then ... but then ...
Life is just a haunting dream.

Edakasi Daniel was born in Pallisa District in Uganda. He is twenty-five years old and is a teacher of English language and literature. He also worked with Sparks News Agency, National Teachers' College Kaliro, as a manager, He is a member of Teso Writers' Foundation and has written over thirty poems and one novel.

GRAINS OF PEACE

A peaceful mind grind rocks of no end.
It starts with your grandfather
And goes to all your ancestral grandchildren.
A peaceful mind unlocks
All the doors of the Chinese temple.
Your culture needs your peace.
Your children need your peace;
You need peace in you.
Don't yearn to splash blood
From your brother's heart.
Don't say,
"After all, my children are not affected."
My children are your children.
You need peace in you
Because it starts with you—
And all your neighbors, friends, and relatives.
So let me educate you:
Harbor peace within you
For your neighbors to have peace.
Believe me,
You will build generations under your thin legs.
And generations will be your peace.

THE GLORY OF A PEN

How do I love you?
What do I feel from you?
Really, can I tell not—
For it's a pain like no
Known ache,
A pain with which I
Would not part, for I
Treasure life—
And life is my heart,
And my heart is yours.
You bring light
Where darkness had sat.
You highlight
Where I come from
And where we are now.
You are not comparable
To the sword.
Yes! Mighty you are—
When I have your might,
Blood of different colors,
I read what's in the world.
I understand not only humanity
But also the sanity of the society.
They are why I ask.

You are my own mighty weapon
That I use for breaking
The wicked and the witches.
I do not have to go to war
To demolish dictatorship and nepotism.
I just used you,
My mighty weapon.
When I write,
They know I am neither happy
Nor contented.
Thus I do mock
As Shakespeare explores.
The pen is mightier than a sword.

DON'T BREAK MY RING

I lay my delicate heart on you:
Let it rise beyond the sky …
And have mercy, never splash it on the floor,
You should enclose me into your ribs.
My heart is a blood pool of River Nile,
Yellow, green, red: all rainbow colors.
Hear my voices across the desert;
Each heartbeat in me echoes miles and miles far;
Across seas, mountains and motionless space.
Rest me between your spread palms.
Take all that I breathe in; or breathe out.
O fairest Valentina!
Never let my heart bleed its blood drops.
You are my last hope; my guiding star.
O, you! whose skin glows like streetlights,
Universe, earth should not see my tears fall down.

CORRUPTION

The elastic stomach—
That stretches from
East to west
Like village catapults!
With money from tax dishes
That the government
Had offer'd to orphans
And widows
To buy cows,
They have eaten wholly,
Wearing corrupt teeth
Like smoking vampires,
Wearing rusted teeth.
Now they are patriotic souls.
See their proboscidial teeth,
Only the beauty of
Yellow or bloody gaps:
Why desire free things?
We buy you cars, tablets,
And fuel, load you
With plenty of allowance,
With national taxes.
Beware of the naked man
Who offers you
Clothes.

UNCHAIN MY HANDS

Good brother, wrong me not, nor wrong yourself.
Make not a bondmaid and slave of me;
That I would disdain. But for these other guards—
Unbind my hands; I'll pull them off myself.
Yea, all my raiment, to my petticoat,
Or what you will command me will I do.
So well I know my duty to my nation.
You jailed me not because I am guilty—
But you called me a suspect.
You asked what I know and what I don't know.
But you have gone on squeezing the bloody chains into my innocent hands.
As I cry, you nod your heads.
Unchain my hands,
At least from outside, before my ground children.
I can neither run nor jump,
But you still deploy heavy security beside me, hungry man,
Like your *man* going to campaign for his flag bearer.
Of course this is not about assassination all over the country,
But his party.
Unchain my hands.

Because you don't know the secret,
You are forced to force me behind the woven bars.
And you focus on my lazy body
As your kids go to bed on empty stomachs.
Please, think far from your shadow, so that you—
Unchain my hands.
For God and my people.

THE BLOOD OF MY LAND

Look at me;
It's a Sunday—
I am on my way to the factory.
This company has become my god:
That's how we live.
You wake up before dawn.
You rub your face with a bit of water
Just to remove the dirt from your eyes.
The month ends.
You are given one hundred thousand.
Rent costs eighty thousand—
Education is worth an infinite amount more.
Day in, day out,
You make doors worth six million a minute—
You get paid six shillings a minute.
And what do you get from it?
If you want to save, then forget eating.

POETRY FROM KENYA

Nancy Ndeke is from the city of Nairobi in Kenya.

"I am an avid reader of works from a wide range of genres. Besides reading, I also write. Poetry is my primary love.

"I have two poetry e-books available from Amazon.com. One is a book of poetry for children, and the other is for an adult audience. The former is a playful game of sounds and words for readers below ten years of age. The latter consists of works covering social injustice in society, love, and many other subjects in between.

"I have also published a novel dealing with societal and systemic injustice amid a struggling economy.

"Last but not least, I have a series in the making, having published the first part. The aforementioned publications are all available at Amazon.com.

"In terms of hobbies, nature is closest to my heart and soul. I find great inspiration in nature. Hence, I find traveling thrilling to my senses."

AFRICA

Teardrops from the sun

Falling onto the sunken cheeks of the son,

He who for centuries

Has known dearth in double portion.

Ships of history felling and ferrying human flesh,

Ankles wired with steel anklets,

Denied name and claim.

You played death games with prayer to alien gods,

Your umbilical cord severed forever ashore.

More!

Even now,

Different game master,

Different elder,

Different player.

Same tools,

Same mission,

Same goals.

And you,

My dear,

Are still missing the piece of the jigsaw.

You plow on with utter blindness

Into treaties of death camps for your own.

Lol!

Does a man hate himself so much as to sell his own for gain?

We blame the news. They love to watch of us wielding machetes to chop up our kin.

Would our cameras shoot a different version?

We blame them for not bringing aid faster when we annihilate entire villages.

Had we thought of the consequences before, would we need it?

We blame them for soiling our forests with depletion.

How did they get the permit?

We blame them for enticing our youths into desert camps for organ harvest.

What are the youth running from back home?

We are as guilty as the warlords with supernova ammo.

We are as guilty as the rapist of our resources seeing we work it together.

Africa!

In your children see the misery painted by disease, hunger, and victimization.

Hear the battle cry of the looters chasing after the innocent.

You have the capacity.

Gather the will.

Return to your senses.

The answer you seek is in your heart.

Moderate your acquisition.

Touch another with kindness.

Rewrite your story for tomorrow with better adjectives.

This perpetual song of woe is tiresome.

Africa!

It is possible to be right and just,

To be guided by the human conscience.

BLEEDING LAND

This here is my land.
This here is Tana,
A river swollen in anger,
Carrying aborted hope down to the sea,
The hopes of scraped wombs upstream,
Uterine walls remain shredded in meatballs of death pieces.
See the rage,
See the pace,
Wildly screaming of rapes, raw and violent,
By blind men with power saws felling cover.
Charcoal merchants' gloomy thievery of riverbanks,
Kenyans watching as fertility flies down the drain,
Awestruck at the bloody massacre of nature.
Who will save this land golden
From holy thieves and christened demons,
Who under cover of godfathers reduce life to graveyards?
Then tomorrow,
Beggar bowls and malnourished children
Shall be breaking news at breakfast shows.
Where is the sanity of the lords of books and caretaker priests?

Tana is speaking.
It has this to say:
"Your greed smells.
Your stupidity stinks.
You have swallowed tomorrow today.
The blood of the innocent unborn is yours,
As is that of the guardians
Who look the other way
As forests upstream scream at rapists at work.
Shame is your lot."

BLESSED CURSE

Come see the maid dark and decked with glittering emeralds,
Standing tall and proud upon a savanna anthill,
Dancing eyes catching the glorious morning sun,
Watching over her father's many head of cattle,
Feeding on the grainfields.
Then comes the blessed visitor,
Winking at the maid and the mother,
Teaching fathers and sons ways of trade,
Of the wealth that lies with the glitterati, taken for granted,
And slimy fluids from the earth worth its weight in gold.
Drums roll.
Roll call for men with an eye for glitter.
Machines make calls like mating birds,
Coughing smoke as another life is pruned.
Friendship of kin has died
At the altar of trade, phony,
Where those divided are divided further,
Each armed to the moon and back with justified hate.
War has come to save a continent.
War has come to kill a continent.
Abroad becomes a reality to many,
Even when abroad is a shallow grave unmarked,
Softening, fresh for old vultures to pick.
The visitor dodges both bullets as he cheers the party on,

Splitting groups into shrapnel of wild militia.
Nightmare has come to stay,
Drinking human blood from morn to night,
With a break to feed the generals in peace
And a chance to rape a teenager recently abducted.
Yes!
It's happening and has been for a while.
The guilty is the owner.
The clean and innocent is the visitor
But pray tell,
Where is the diamond at the center of the conundrum?
Where is the gold bullion from the Congo's forest fields of massacres?
Libya has its story true and denied.
For wrestling with gods, their homes were destroyed and chiefs deposed.
No one, of course, talks of Iraq.
Who could?
A fancy term of springing desert dwellers.
It was a justified case in any case, right?
Answers abide.
Where is the crude oil from South Sudan's fields of slaughter?
Gone! Going! And still going,
With the hidden hand that gives and takes,
Yet removed from the conflict by way of deniability.
Count your losses, Africa, and realize this:
Your only true friend is perhaps your Creator,
Not the multinationals building roads to steal with ease,
Not the enslavers wearing sunny smiles,
Not the moneylenders collecting your children's souls in war zones.
Not all blessings are blessings.
Some blessings are curses in disguise.

BONES

Scattered haphazardly across the African plains,
Bones tell a story deeply buried.
They sing dirges in shallow graves,
Pointing fleshless fingers toward the setting sun.
They ask answers for questions that died in infancy.
Grass refuses to grow.
Flowers bend their heads in shameful tears.
Bones!
Stubborn remains of corporeal enterprises—
Bones!
Rocky smiles of broken teeth, of milk teeth,
From slave trade days,
With empire thundering its wild hooves around the ocean's beaches,
To rapes of highlands to feed egos and mistresses.
Bones!
Echo of the dead and dying,
Falling one at a time,
In fields marked for exploration.
Bones!
Seen in the transparent children pregnant with hunger,
Bones!
Of elders slowly rotting in shanty establishments miles away from homes,
Bones!

Of youth fighting a war they can never win,
Bones!
Of unborn bastards of nightly visits of men wild with revengeful libidos.
The story of Africa.
The story of bones.
Bones, tons of bones.
From the north in its desert expanse,
Crude oil chases the timid inhabitant with raining bombs.
From the east sponsored war destabilizes millions to harvest more crude.
From the central region,
The land of gems and teak forests,
Death is predictable.
The west has its own demons of mutated creed,
Teaching abduction of underage lasses
To score payments and sow their wild oats.
Africa!
The land of monumental bones.
See Rwanda's heap, its proud pile of genocide skulls!
The eagle lives high up the cliffs,
Directing fishing of bones across the continent,
The loot divided in offshore accounts on islands a thousand miles away.
Africa!
The guilty thief is your bosom friend,
The conniving robber is your mentor,
The rogue terminator is your advisor.
O Africa!
How long shall you remain blind!
How long shall you remain deaf!
When will you change your selection of those you do business with?
When will you filter the CVs of those you invite to invest?
When will you say no if yes means the death of your kin?
Africa!
Weigh friendships,
Discern the morality of your colleagues,

Evaluate the offers for you and your people.
Their humility is a tent,
Hoarding evil in canned proposals.
Their smile is that of a hyena.
Your death is a feast to them.
Their handshake is a stamp.
To share in the shame that leaves your people impoverished,
Africa!
Are you proud of bones staring at you?
The battering of your people daily?
Look in the eye of the friend with offered gifts.
Those gifts have killed.
They shall continue to kill,
Till the truth you get,
That in negotiations,
The devil is in the details,
And the details are the scattered bones across your plains,
The cry of rivers running with shed blood,
Refugee status for your people,
Diseased populations,
Unschooled youths.
For the hand of your friends is awash with a hidden agenda,
An agenda to benefit himself
At your expense.
Greed has no manners;
Greed has no calling;
Greed has no gentlemen;
Greed has no qualms about murder.
That is he whom you do business with,
The business of bones in display and continuing.
Enough is just enough.
It is now!

DANCE

Come dance with colors,
Red the primary rose in dust,
Red the glow of streaming life,
Red the flow of the ebbing tide of souls.
Bask under the colorful sky.
Say a quick prayer before the burst of pink blossoms,
Summary of life soon seethed with smoke.
Run in circles till you drop.
Bears and eagles in coitus of arrhythmic sex,
Cheered on by stripes and emblems of cousins.
Dance the seismic epileptic twirl,
Hugging hope with its broken ropes.
Hang on even as you are hung.
Tease death with tenacious sighs.
Heaven has come on a familiar road.
Friends and foes in contest brawl.
Powers of propaganda machines at full throttle.
Who is wrong, who is right,
As men take sides according to gods,
And women stand beside their men in denial and applause?
Mess is meddling, and confusion ascends the throne.
Each truth is told differently;
Each lie is pieced indifferently.
Usher in a new era.

Who shall be left standing when wisdom and foolishness are drunk with lies?
Come dance to a dark night filled with the beauty of death.
Count breaths before taking roll call.
Anyone answering is dead.
The living are busy dying,
Survivors clapping for winners and losers,
As looters and loiterers lunge forward, carrying sacks of nothingness,
But their broken spirits in torn baskets.
War has color.
Not the type that builds.

DEVIL'S PRICE

In the marketplace,
Where all has been for sale for millennia,
Tears flow in tidal waves.
Hiccups of broken voices rumble, thunderous.
Flashes of bombs and muzzle guns dispensing master schemes.
Africa,
Cannon fodder for all and sundry,
Your sky is the bluest invitation for death flights,
Your deserts home to infants gasping for air,
Your forests drawing queer and straight for a turn to rape,
Your cities blue-chip gambler dens for rogue advisors.
Africa!
Who cursed you and forgot to reverse the curse?
What others get to celebrate,
You get to mourn.
Resources attracting goons like vultures smelling rot.
See your oil fields, dear dark man,
From Nigeria, to Libya, to South Sudan.
See the desolation met upon your people,
Ghost homes sighing with the burden of the crude slime that *must* be stolen.
From Congo, to Mali, to Somalia,
See shame shelters roofed with torn plastic sheets, heating up your broken souls in refugee camps,

Haggard looks staring vacantly at nothing,
Your maids selling their bony flesh for a stale doughnut,
Your sons smoking weed to deal with the demons of boredom,
Your wives commonplace entertainment for every Tom with a dick and a gun.
Ha!
Africa!
Can't you recognize the trader in the devil, or is it the devil in the trader?
Once you sold your youth to slavery to a mercantile system to grow cotton and sugarcane.
Sex via rape was a thrown-in bargain for those who survived the rough seas and starvation.
Round one it was—
Or was it round seven, dear?
Your son helped carry the crucifixion tree for the Messiah.
Was that Simon or …?
That was perhaps the fourth, or eighth, or tenth.
Who could keep count of your toxic mistreatment, dear?
Experiments to determine the viability of drugs are done on rats and your sons.
Ha!
Africa!
What is it you owe the devil? Will you not once and for all pay?
All the diamonds and gold in the bowels of your land.
For you the reward is sponsored terrorism and "warlordism."
Uganda had "Saint" Joseph Kony terrorizing the people for decades on end,
Supporting his evil mission with blood diamonds, gold, and teak logs from your forests.
He was more armed than the government, even the UN.
Ha!
The one who arms you arms him.
How about that for business, eh!
And who could that be, dear sleeping, mourning Africa?!

Now it's Boko Haram in Nigeria.
Girls fetched from classrooms to keep generals and lieutenants warm in the bush,
Arrogant enough to return them with a couple of kids.
Government army humbled by bigger, heavier weaponry from the bush.
Ha!
Africa, who is fooling whom here?
They say it's the sons of Abraham carrying old grudges.
Is it true, or are you carrying a myth to justify mayhem?
Did any mention Somalia and the al-Shabaab nightmare?
ISIS is the current term.
Skinning heads of their captives before tying them to the backs of Land Cruisers, dragging them along till their flesh and bones mix with the sandy paths.
Ha!
Africa, dear, who will mourn your last man standing?
Nairobi!
The city of the sun built on the place of sweet waters.
Politics has lasted a year to elect a leader,
Politics of food, politics of principals, politics of tribe, politics of regions and greed and corruption.
But
Could it be that crude currently being drilled in the northern frontier is the issue at hand?
Could it be?
A national resistance movement even got born in the process,
The newborn armed to the teeth by guardian grandpas.
Too early to say, but the ominous clouds hover.
Ha!
Africa,
What do you owe the devil, dear,
That your children scatter in the winds of hunger,
While arable fertile lands lay fallow?
What do you owe the devil, dear,

That your people are housed in dilapidated refugee camps in dusty corners of neighboring countries?
While another is paid, there is the price of a small hill and lake to make reports of your dying process.
Ha!
Africa,
See foreign shores awash with the bloated bodies of your women and children,
All having attempted to flee the ready death at home, only to end with speedy death in capsized boats or shot-up boats.
Ha!
Africa, dear,
Your children sell their organs to raise funds to escape their homes,
Only for harvesters to pick that which is sold and all else.
When is enough really ever enough?
What do you owe the devil that he camps in your beautiful dark continent?
What's the price you must pay to be free, dear?
Only truth, dear mother Africa, may save you,
The truth that your benefactor is other than good and must meet scrutiny before allowed in,
Only truth that not all deals build (most break),
Only truth that corruption eats the corrupt and the innocent,
Only truth that you are being taken advantage of by those saintly, soft-spoken merchants of death,
Truth that no amount of faith can change the status quo, but your singular determination for the greater good of your people can.
Ha!
Africa,
From the accounts of history,
If you ever owed,
The debt is long paid,
Even if by no one else but
By the son of Cyrene who bore the cross of Christ.

As for the war of "Abrahamic" siblings,
You would be a fool to become entangled in a brotherhood affair.
So rise in truth and look deep into your own souls.
There lies the truth of your people's salvation.
Scrutinize the offered hand of deals,
Not its color but its intentions.
If it smells ratty, it is ratty
And can only woe bring,
As centuries have shown.

LIVING

Living is beyond breath, *way* beyond!
Striving is familiar territory for the masses in Africa.
Beauty fades fast, *way* faster than a rose in the dead of winter,
Gambling in open casinos where the chips are the poor searching for a morsel
And the gambler is any with a false promise and a purse full.
Tentacles thrive
To ensnare the unsuspecting vulnerable ones.
Poverty drives their broken lives with the force of a hurricane,
Pushing them into the ready hands of two-legged hyenas and insatiable vultures.
Running is the mainstay of all still breathing.
From warring clans they run,
From cultural animosities they run,
From invading goons under others' employ they run,
From hunger they run,
From disease they run.
"Run, run, run" is the daily chorus for many.
Tribal wars chase,
Corruption in nations chases,
Illiteracy also chases,
Low incomes do chase,
Joblessness for sure chases.
"Run, run, run" is the daily chorus for many.

Hitting walls of repression daily,
Hitting tunnels of visionless hope daily,
Hitting mental agony borne of desperation daily;
"Run, run, run" is the daily chorus for many.
Yet,
Upon this vast continent,
Classes do live beyond dreams of fairies.
Largesse is their emblem every day.
They flash their health and wealth in statements of fashion display.
Their homes are traveled abroad several times over.
Basking in the glory of ill-gotten proceeds
While in cahoots with land rapists.
Large masses get pushed beyond living to graveyards.
Survivors are driven like cattle into refugee camps
Here, restlessness rules the coop.
Morals are exchanged for cheap underwear.
Slowly, with the passage of years, wrong becomes right.
Back where they came from,
Pipes sprout up into giant refineries,
Drilling in superdrive.
Rich thugs wedded to aspiring rich thugs.
To ensure the owners don't ever return,
Sporadic wars are displayed every once in a while,
With media frenzy carrying the news to the camps.
Mystery of wars and conflicts carry each day,
Burying fear deep into the unborn child's DNA.
Giving up is then the availed option.
It's not unheard of for such displaced to be placed elsewhere,
Elsewhere oceans apart,
Where everything is new and distant, including their supplanted hearts.
Their carried dislike soon becomes hate.
They brood anger, soon bleeding animosity,
And vengeance is no longer a far distance to carry,
But a subject held dear by a population no longer alive but "alive."

These are goats all sacrificed at the altar of greed.
All these are lesser humans preyed on by their fellow men.
And the lands breed ceaselessly.
From all corners of this continent,
Mayhem, drums, roll calls of fighting, killing, maiming, massacres, genocides, terrorism, and civil wars,
Resulting in a familiar pattern.
Democracy and rights are the excuses.
Reasons are other than what is stated.
And the cycle continues,
Pitting wild men in dark suits playing wild jazz against uniformed goons.
Bush wars and economy wars bite the poor twice.
Death rules this land,
From prostitution by choice to flesh peddling by proxy,
From slavery of the youth by con artists to sex slaves by gentlemen with money bags.
Guilt drips incessantly down the valleys and plains of men of faith.
Groups exist to help themselves at the expense of others.
Even creed is neutered into acquiescence by the powers that be.
This land bleeds! O how it bleeds!
And the tragedy of this bleeding diarrhea is the owners and foreigners in cahoots,
So who speaks for the victims?
Who but the same demon speaking the local tongue in reversal?
Africa!
Look within your bloated stomach for the answers you seek.

In the piled-up fat and hunger the truth lies.
You are the problem and the solution held in both hands.
All you need is strength not to sell your soul,
Like you have done for centuries now,
And as still do in shameless abandon,
Welcoming marauders into your families
To sweep your children into so many hungers.
It's no wonder they die en masse.
Run! Running to nowhere farther away than an early grave.

MEMORIES

Age, distance, and preoccupation
Have turned not the sight
Of soldiers of each divide,
Facing off.
The captives tied up
In grotesque positions,
Sweat and fear etched on their faces.
The victors
Soundlessly kindling a fire
With logs huge,
Flames licking the hot afternoon sky.
They picked two—
One young,
One older—
And threw them, tied, into the blaze.
The horror of their screams
Carried a distance.
Captors smiling and laughing in glee,
Others jumping in joy,
The captives whimpering on the side,
Helplessness keeping them impotent,
Till noises died down.
Corpses sizzling red with human fat dripping,
Sending bluish smoke into the air:

Human roast!
The burning heads burst, releasing held memories.
Time stood still
Then.
"*Eat!*"
Shouted the leader.
With quaking hands
And labored breath,
They consumed, albeit hesitantly,
Their colleagues under armed supervision.
Then,
The seven were shot dead,
Point-blank range,
And only
One was released to share the horror of their captivity
With those of his side
Who could with certainty deny
The evil in humankind.
Who can say for sure humans are human
And not bedeviled by evil beyond what's comprehensible.
I know not.
The true insanity of the world
Is most prominent in war and conflict.
To see it and hear it and live it.

O MOSES!

Come, strike this steel tap and give me water.
The Nile is fishing guerrillas and militias.
Pharaoh and Pharisees line the banks,
Throwing rockets and bazookas all day long.
Come stammer to the valley of death.
Bring up bitter drops. I shall oblige.
I don't want to die before I live,
O Moses!
Come reason with oilmen,
Those who my land they took,
Chasing me abroad to rot in camps,
My cattle dried up in drought forced,
My children with another they call father.
O Moses!
Come strike the milkmen blind,
Those who rob children of childhood,
Making them make children unprepared,
Paying them with disease and plagues.
Those who protest drink a raw bullet.
O Moses!
Won't you come and bring down the manna?
Hunger has grown roots in Africa.
Remember not the slavery but the pumpkins
That fed your folk for four hundred years.

Forgive and lend a handful of seeds,
And tell Pharaoh to release his stranglehold on the Nile.
O Moses!
Is yours a myth of snakes?
Come swallow the python and vipers aplenty.
They eat the crop, the sower, and the tractor,
Pounding the land with smoking chariots at speed.
Death is now a full-grown adult.
He feeds on tons of skulls on a bad day.
On a good day it's called genocide.
O Moses!
Won't you mark their doors?
And send drones at night till we cross these poverty lines?
O Moses!
Write some more commandments.
Add revenge—one you forgot to include—
Add mischief so robbery is canonized.
Add insults so vulgarity is official.
Add wars in rapid succession around the globe.
O Moses!
Won't you legalize crime unfair,
Add murder for population control?
Add!
O Moses!
Add everything wrong so the playing field becomes level.
For since you crashed the commandments,
We break the smaller pieces into yet more pieces with glee.
O Moses!
Come and get stoned by stoned protesters of the law,
Especially if you don't strike this tap for water,
The fluid the coming war is all about.
O Moses!
Come before they come for you.

POTTERS

The sojourners are in an alien land,
Groaning under the weight of their tasks,
Some man-made,
Some God-ordained.
Bowls that hold momentary journeys of living,
Sources of mighty rivers,
Who sip with grudges cultural,
King minders before wings sprout with power,
Givers.
Unsung heroines of balance,
Teaching preachers,
Nursing maids.
Yet
The world unkind is,
Pollutes her very existence,
In dim denials and much hurt.
Her kind, her kin,
Belittle, betray,
Relegating them to shadow,
Cornering them with rude rides
From corner to corner,
Distant or near.
Her fate is tears held with scorn.
Mothers smothered with vitriol by sons,

Sisters devoiced with harsh glares by fathers.
Eve is crying.
She wails.
She asks,
"Why, O seed of my womb?
What's my lot in cultural insults
That break the very pot that carries your life?"
From ashore tender hearts get deflowered.
In other places they tuck them into the back.
Some are sold as cattle to a butcher.
What is her crime in the ones she births?
Walking in the footsteps of those before her,
Mimicking strength while burdened by the reckless mistreatment of her children,
A woman is a human,
Without whom even the homosexual has no partner.
A woman is human,
Vital as vital means to humanity.
The section that segregates her
Is one that wounds itself.
They are the completeness of life.

POVERTY

There is nothing poetic in poverty.
There is nothing praiseworthy about hunger,
Or disease,
Or homelessness.
Like war scars,
They are emotional challenges
Best mitigated with sound policy
And a willing sincerity,
Not charms and amulets.
Poor folks' prevention against malaria.
Ignorant prevention against malnutrition.
See the ghetto scene,
How refuse flows green with raw feces,
Cholera sinking children and elders.
See the distended tummies of rickety survivors,
Black charms wound around skeletal waists
To ward off evil eyes and witches.
But pray tell this:
What's the purpose if tomorrow the child is dead anyway?
More births in quick succession.
Half die young.
Survivors are burnt alive in botched robberies.
Then weep and gnash teeth
At evil eyes as we Africans do,

Ignoring truth glaring.
Ignorance is disease cursed.
As long as you believe so, it shall be.
Witchcraft the excuse for all your ills.
Who shall tell this story with a better ending?
Health care and education are not campaign tools,
But basic needs to stem the perennial flow of tears.
Throw the charms down the stench hole;
Throw the amulets into the rubbish pit.
The solution lies elsewhere.
Food and Medicare are magic for health.
Breeding rats is the business of rats.
Humans would have a better chance to live better
If only ignorance were not such bliss
For those who know the value but keep it close.
So the world laughs and scoffs at us,
Counting sixteen births to a skeletal female,
Politicians counting votes from the dying voters,
Praying they live long enough to vote.
Our problems are indeed uniquely ours.
Shame of cultures that engender meekness,
Not questioning what fells your own.
Yet international meets are held in your cities,
Pass resolutions to favor the poor
Who die en masse encased with charms and amulets.
Shame is the name of this sordid game.
Tragedy is its synonym.
Evil is its twin in war,
Born of conflicts building on the ignorance of Africa's people.

RAISE HOPE

For all in need,
Be it child or man,
Lend a hand,
Be it beast or tree,
Lend a hand.
Wrap a gauze of love around the bleeding wounds of neglect.
Wrap an arm of gentle hug around the wailing souls in agony.
The world hurts so.
The land is filled with woe,
With resounding bludgeoned bitterness.
Look how the unborn writhe in pain.
Look how the pregnant run in hate,
Pouring acidic perfumes on the heads of infants.
Hell arrives in droves at doorsteps,
Claiming and dispossessing the deserts.
If not Congo tonight, then it's Syria today.
The Rohingya people have not healed.
South Sudanese are calling from half-buried positions.
Mali has its melee to meet,
Nigeria, the great African giant, is bleeding with its maids as bait for warlords.
Ha!
How hyenas laugh with glee.
Even the weather groans from the forcing hands of rapists.

Forests wish to run from the madness of marauding man,
But where?
Desert creeps to the highlands, clapping.
Mountain sheds its crop of bamboo to mean cowboys.
Rivers wink in their diminishing glory;
They wither and sink into the drought earth.
Death roams our world.
War is the constant,
Over lands and resources.
Greed is the common denominator.
Boasting of weapons of mass destruction.
Daily shows of mighty men showing off their nuclear balls.
Life becomes a never-ending storm,
Blowing us thither and nowhere.
O how earth cries.
Who shall lend a hand to mitigate?
Who shall preach to the deaf war robots?
Who shall teach the rogue rulers of the dignity of life?
It's you!
You,
In your assumed smallness,
Raise your voice as the flag of hope.
Perhaps sense may return.
Raise your flag of hope for the world.
You owe it.

SOME FACTS

Are hard to accept
When heard from the other side.
Pregnant at thirteen
From the loins of Moses the cow boss,
Bought to feed the hunger
Of a family devoid of means.
A mother blessed your teary journey
To the rape house by a giant custodian of culture.
The baby cried.
You too cried.
To instill sense of motherhood in one so green,
He banged your head hard enough to crack your jaw.
Older wives laughed at your tragedy. You suckled the master's son.
One year later,
Another mound shows.
Seven pregnancies in ten years.
You!
Only three and twenty,
But wizened and wrinkly, bent over a buttress,
Groaning under the weight as vodka fumes strike home with a fiery stench.
Who shall plead your case even as he lies dead?
Immediate arrangements for inheritance having been made already.
The night after the funeral,

Another marathon you cried,
With the eldest son taking claim of you.
O! Blessed daughter of a pauper,
Yours is the fact of a teary path.
Unable to leave,
Loving the brood you bore,
You died at thirty,
An old hag broken of spirit,
The clan counting in glory
Your seven emaciated sons,
Worth every skinny cow paid for you at thirteen.
Your spirit free but not those of your daughters,
Born of a slave culture,
Where girl-children are mere factories of pleasure and childbearing.
Such a shame in this day and age.

STAIN

Am small, oh so small.
Not for long if my father's picture remains true.
Am poor, oh so poor.
My uncle calls me a stain on the family,
For Father brought a worm home
That ate my mother and baby sister.
Am confused, oh so confused,
At the hurt flung at me by other kids.
Am embarrassed, oh so embarrassed,
By my threadbare uniform unique.
I hung out at back to hide the missing part.
I bow down low to evade the teacher's sharp rebuke,
But I must this school attend, stain name or not.
I must these lessons take, embarrassed or not.
Against all odds, I must learn,
Learn, learn till drunk I get of learning.
Run, run with the books till shame of my paupery dims.
If I must die from hunger before graduation,
Let it not be said I didn't try.
But I try and try again amid cries.
I will soldier on till I rest with winners,
Work my mind and hands till my shame fades.
For those who wrote me off, I will forgive.
For my uncle's and others' kind abuse and scorn, I shall forgive.

For kids name-calling and teachers speaking in rough tongues I shall forgive.
For I will be so busy living that I promise to forget.
But this I shall forget not:
The one who give me a meal warm,
The one who stopped and wiped my tears,
The one who gave an old shirt,
Plus the one who saved me from rich bullies.
Am only a child with a dream.
What's my crime for being an orphan?
I promise *myself* this:
If school will lead me out of poverty,
I shall die learning,
Even if at the back of the group I stand.
Poverty steals no dreams.
Cowardice does that,
And that I have not.

THE OTHER CHILD

Like a bug
In the king's walls,
Squashed with no qualms.
Ride him hard.
Slash him too.
None shall cry for him,
His cry being mute
And you powerful.
Circle his homestead.
Close the doors.
Lob a bomb,
Burying evidence with the charred remains.
Why not!
"He is the other child
Of the other man,
Of lesser gods."
Africa!
The land of experimental evil.
From drugs to policy to polity,
From weapons to poisons to prisons,
Try it all,
And while you're at it,
Take in return
The youths, who are easy pickings, to serve as slaves.

The learned in their learnedness can be bought with land proceeds.
The powers that be!
Alas!
Teach them the math of thieves,
Which is misery added to hunger equals obedience.
Then together,
You can rape the land in glee,
Cover your tracks with human faces,
An orphanage here, a refugee camp there,
Food trucks loaded with vitamins,
Colored books for the illiterate masses to stare at.
If more noise,
Change the tune for the old marching song.
Douse them with fumes at night, and bury the balance alive.
Africa!
Where trade is murder and mayhem.
Africa!
Where birth is condemnation.
Africa!
Where death is no longer news.
The united world watches from a distance,
One hand in the spoils,
One hand soothing the militia;
One hand preaching peace,
One hand raised to strike.
Africa!
No!
There is such a thing as enough.
There is such a thing as enough.
And now,
Your children have suffered enough.
Say no to bullying priests.
Say no to stealing saints.
Say no to friends with benefits,

For they no longer serve you.
But their distended stomachs
Like the great canyon keep yawning for more blood.
Africa!
There is such a thing as decency and honor.
Look for those qualities in the friends you make.

UNTITLED (THIS BLEEDING BABY)

Gently touch this bleeding baby.
Her heart, as yet immature, pity.
She pleads in silence deep,
Lost in the great unfeeling labyrinth of an abandoned careless orphanage,
Her fate that of a soldier captured behind enemy lines,
An entertainment vessel for her supposed caregiver.
Her nights are long, oh so long!
The shadow shafts again and again, drilling unfailing.
Feet dead, limbs numb, blisters ripe.
Pain is a second skin.
The caregiver is now the tear giver, remorseless,
Preying on the praying child.
Where is God, who took her mommy to a better place?
Where is the Lord who loved her daddy more than she did?
Where are the angels who took her big brother to the heavenly choirs to sing for God?
No answer,
Not yet,
But night is drawing fast.
Faster too,
The caregiver, now tear giver, is restless to start the onslaught.
Who will hear the silent plea of this baby?

At eight years and a month,
She dreams of death though she understands it not.
She knows hate though she cannot explain it.
She remembers not what love was.
Not cookies, not cartoons funny,
Can dim the pangs of horror in wait
If he comes tonight.
That's the news of the next day,
That a child was killed under unclear circumstances,
That a child escaped after this heinous crime,
That a child was armed with a blunt knife,
That a child was an orphan under the excellent care of a faith-based institution,
Or so the newsmen howl.
Who will tell the child's story?
Who will tell of the child's nights?
Who will tell of the child's life that was no life?
Quick to believe, quick to veil evil,
The director issues scathing attacks on the child,
Her ingratitude stealing the show time hour.
But the child cares not;
She lies in rest forever
On the dumpster site a mile to the east.
The dead speaks louder than the living.
Her tattered body tells what killed the caregiver.
Did it have to end this way?

THE POET'S POT

The poet's pot is broken,
Its water dripping, seeping deep into the dark unknown,
Running,
Racing away fast from enemies of life,
Hiding honey way away into the unreachable,
Shyly blinking in shame for the onslaught visited by "friends."
Water,
Source and sustainability of living,
Now teardrops fought over by flies.
A story of abidance, abundance, weak in faint.
Water,
Earth's mother goddess,
Trampled and suffocated daily,
Take flight to escape wasted rocks,
Take a dive to deflect wasted acids,
Now a carrier made by all starting with kids,
Professional water masters peddling drops of pollution,
Carrying home poison for slow intimate death.
Water,
Once without thought never majored,
Now wars are in paper stages, waiting, waging,
As boys skip school to lend a gallon hand,
As mothers hoard a few drops for the sick at night.
This is a journey into a desert of warring tribes.

We all walk blindly, led by our unseeing leaders,
Into the Waterloo of waterless basins
By earthlings who shoot the golden geese.
With parched throats,
We should practice the dying chorus,
Blaming nature for our own faulty living.
Water.
Life.
Or
War and *death*.

WEEPING WILLOWS

This giant that snores nonstop,
Bleeding relentlessly, over and over,
Calling in silenced weeping,
Culture rich, dragging you along,
Traditions eloquent with generosity,
Hands upraised in beggary and deity praise,
The witch and wizard aboard your shaky boats,
Peeling oranges ripe and grapes purple with succulent juice,
Your own dining on the peels and husks with swine.
Why?
O why, Mother Africa,
Aren't we to learn anything from history?
So daily we weave poetry stories topped with tears.
Humility is virtue, not servitude.
You lend a hand after filling your tummy.
You!
O Mother Africa!
Why dance the devil's dance, selling your birthright?
You smile with milk teeth at the coyotes eating your chicks,
You tango with demons drilling holes into your future,
Your baskets full to overflowing with emptiness,
Your granaries saturated with aborted hope.
See how your tomorrow tumbles in death fields.
See how your maids grovel on foreign soils pregnant with disease.

Your elders hurriedly rush to graves with shame,
The wombs of your women ripped open for vultures to pick.
Why, oh why, this blind immoral sowing of grand malpractice?
The foreign friend heaping abuse on you is no guiltier than your bloodied hand.
The thief and the watcher are thieves.
The jailed and the jailer live in jail.
O Africa!
When shall your tune change?
When shall your chorus change?
When shall hummed dirges change for a sunny disposition?
You have a responsibility to yourself.
Only then,
Death mother,
Can true change for good embrace your children
And halt the weeping willows that dot your backyards.

IMPORTED ANSWERS

This is the soil where trials have built castles.
This the land of oil rebukes and diamond madness,
The land of gold tempests and slavery hymns,
The land where questions gather like winter storms,
Asking but the right one,
Where disease curable is the bane of child mortality
And more deaths are registered per thousand than anywhere else.
Where the locals know more about things international,
Visitors get fed fat and cream, while the malnourished perish in ghettos,
Malaria has been at war with the folks,
Each season claiming millions.
But we must wait—O we must!—
For the imported vaccine to reach a corner without roads.
We must wait for multivitamins to reach a village marooned at the forest's edge.
We must wait for body bags to hide our myriad dead.
And clapping shall thunder after the tender given
To supply grains late for the starving,
The foreigners pocketing the cash, the grain, and the profit
Who cursed land of my father
To bear only sons with appetites for blood,
To raise rogue daughters selling the land for gems,
To pick priests with an appetite for child abuse,
To employ a leadership of men of warring tendencies?

Your story is hard to tell,
Just as your history is hard to tell.
You are the disease of your people.
The doctor is the disease of his people.
He harvests your living organs with your help.
Isn't this insanity?
The mole in your head digs deeper.
Your conscience dies like an old tree standing.
It's time not to keep silent.
It's time to call it as it is.
Corruption eats from within like a mole,
Unless it is plucked in spite of the pain of shame.
Africa!
The imported solutions you wallow in
Are impotent illusions you dwell in.
Wake up and let the truth of your compromise live out.

THOMAS

He says that until he sees it, it exists not,
So climate change is an old wives' tale
To confuse progress with digress.
He says that global warming is a fairy tale,
That pundits sell expressly to while time
And scare away the harvesters of logs and oil reserves.
So April has come with a weird gift,
Storms unknown to this land since Mau Mau claimed it from his pale brother.
So a storm came:
Thunder, usual,
No snow, unusual.
At the belt of the equator they lay,
Harvesting unripe coffee beans from the loaded bushes,
Shredding banana plantains into ribbons lacy.
Shock and dismay is the farmer's horror gaze,
He to whom the story of climate change is alien.
But you who should know care not an ounce
When winds uproot a cash crop from the ground,
The entire mainstay of poor folks,
Who grow your beans, sweet coffee.
How in heaven and hell alike do you claim responsibility
For warming the earth with your wanton greed?
These are signs ominous.

Who's to say tomorrow the mountain won't move
To the sea in anger, sweeping all in its wake?
It's appalling, it's irresponsible.
No other way of calling men with knowledge
But who degrade the earth because they can.
Poor folks getting poorer till the poor call them poor.
Shame is the lot of those duly dallying in denial
Like Thomas of yore,
While scars stare you in the face as facts.
Global warming is a reality grim.

NANCY

Mother!
You have fruits aplenty, dear.
Your children drenched in scabies can't stop the itch.
You have grains bounteous, but
Your children keel over in hunger.
You have rubies and jade, but
Your children strut the alleys in tattered hand-me-downs.
You have rivers and swamps to grow tubers, but
Your children carry kwashiorkor pregnancies to full term.
You have plains rich in wildlife, but
Your children poach with reckless abandon for others' gain,
Five fingers pointing abroad.
Who plays ball alone?
You hold down your children's legacy for another to loot,
Content with a little kickback stupidity.
You break off plots of rich land through eviction
To pave the way for glory malls and toxic industries.
Is it a curse or pus that our minds harbor?
Is it a brainwash or a brain flood with humus?
Is it ideology or moronic inclination
That we borrow the worst from the worst,
That we copy the sloppy from the sloppiest,
That we ape the fakery from the fakest,
Who to change this sewer flow stench?

However hard you groan,
From within seek guidance with your own sense.
Your cry thunders to the shock of the world.
Heal yourself, dear.
And if you do indeed need aid,
Ask for lessons moral,
Ask for direction straight,
Ask for prayer earnest,
Ask for wise direction.
For the shame of suffering with so much
Is shame total,
For you are partner to your crime.

SWEET DIVIDE

Here's the law
That rules the land for all,
Blind to color, blind to race,
Informed soldiers, uniformed soldiers,
Fighting, righting wrongs fair,
Till
Pockets are turned inside out.
Gold lined with diamond buttons
Till
Offshore accounts and numbered accounts are numbered.
Let the best man win in the law race.
Legal and illegal dance in a twirl.
Evidence takes a walk to the beach for a swim.
Material witness rushes for a well-earned holiday.
Judge takes off to nurse assumed injuries.
Prosecutor reads from an old misplaced paper:
"Postpone.
Postpone."
News tires of waiting.
The poor one robbed waits.
He waits for justice to crawl out of recess.
A year.
Two years.
Gong strikes.

New evidence.
Start of old case.
One, two, three, seven years.
Poverty drives the victim to the grave.
No case.
No complainant.
Case closed.
Bravo.
Justice won the day.
Who could argue against such an impeccable show of pursuit of justice?
No.
Case closed.
Justice served.
Evil is paid top dollar.
Good is buried.
Hurray!
Transparency lives in the opaque services
Provided by paid justice.
Death served the complainant,
As someday
It will serve the usurper of justice.
But until then,
Shame on those who subvert justice
Just because.
Karma will sort you out.
Trust the poet who says the same
About the sweet divide of law.

FREIGHT

Above the said and implied
Is the real and visible,
The soul of an engine
Running on hope.
Aloft, above,
Seeing the clouds close,
Catching a whiff of scent
From borders long and far,
Comeliness stays,
In hearts thrums,
Awaits the ladder
To fly the shore,
All else dimming.
Staggered thoughts scatter,
Leaving nakedness of nature.
Calling shots in short spurts,
Distance is a mirage.
Reality is a dream of a soul;
Desire is a driver.
Hope has wings.
Faith is a rock.
Come into this future already here.
Sample the rainbow's spice,
Build a home of breath silk,

Tell the wind to softly touch.
You are where you deem.
You shall live where your heart so chose.
Up above, here below,
Life is for the living and daring.
Tests are parable's real.
Impossible is a threat to any faith.
Miracles are daily meals.
Come into your own, on terms your own.
Walk the air with gait guarantee.
Seek your own counsel before others'.
Still the fears that rule lesser men by their poor choices.
Be at one with your Creator's glory.
You are meant to be more.
Don't limit yourself;
Not all winged birds fly.
The elephant has a soft walk.
Listen to your own fancy.
Hold a meeting with yourself.
Lead yourself home.
Company is great when sought,
Not you to complete,
But you to complement,
For the universe is you in you.
So come fly;
See the glory of your ability.
In gratitude lift another.
Love is lonely if for oneself alone.
So come, let's fly,
And let laughter ring loud beyond the borders
That decimate in the presence of true humanity
Such as I and you.

Benjamin Chelangat was born in Kenya in 1989 and was raised in Uganda, where he studied from primary level to the university level. He is a graduate of English literature from Kyambogo University. He currently works with the Teachers Service Commission of Kenya as a classroom teacher.

Benjamin is a poet who is alive to the fact that Africa has to a great extent ceased to develop because of the greed for power of some leaders, corruption, nepotism, tribalism, and civil wars. He believes that by using his poetic pen as a weapon, he will be in a position to shoot down some excesses that have for years reduced Africa to being an object of ridicule. His poem "Buried without Graves" was inspired by his urge to unravel the consequences of wars not only in Africa but also across the whole world.

BURIED WITHOUT GRAVES

On the mountaintop,
fire spoke
the language of no return:
of thunder and boom!

They were buried without graves,
without the teary vigil
that would console the bereaved …
"Take heart. God loved them more."
Heroes, yet gone;
soldiers, yet lifeless
in the alien bushes,
where death is a friend.

They were buried without graves
in the land where bullets pass the sentence
from the arena of mortality.

Buried without graves
in the foe's territory,
yet hailed back home
for impregnating the general's bank account
with the leaves of the world.

They were buried without graves
by the wild, joyous scavengers
who performed the funeral
in the jungles
without the church hymns
to appease the departing souls to the world without end.

The fallen heroes
have rested in pieces,
exterminated by those they do not hate,
while dancing to the orders of those they do not love.
Now, they rest without graves
in the land that is never their home.

Philip Mainge is from Kenya.

DYING AFRICA

The trend by which Africa takes on its sociopolitical agenda is always worrying and unpredictable. For the last sixty-one years, things has gone from good to worse! Some African countries have the grim tendency to love dictatorship—a trend that has gone underestimated but that now is showing its ugly head.

Ghana was the first African nation to gain freedom from its oppressors, the French. But it never took long before their leader was killed. This created a new wave of democracy in Africa, where leaders agreed to disagree. And this stopped economic growth. Why? Because no development can take place when the worrisome political parties have own their people killing each other via armed militia, for example, the Rwanda genocide. There is always a wave of ethnicity and tribalism that gnaws the leadership day after day.

In West Africa, especially Nigeria, there were coups d'état, one after another, and this, no doubt, slowed down the nation's social, political, and economic development. Moreover, the neighboring nations followed suit, and a series of coups d'état became sort of an everyday affair. Indeed this was one way of retarding economic growth. The developed nations such as some European countries, Germany, Japan, China, and the United States did not wish to venture into such places. If they did, they needed to use their ambassadors to monitor the situation before they ventured into the business of starting industries and so forth.

However, all the nations ruled by Great Britain and Germany—for example, Uganda and Kenya—did not indulge in coup d'état. Even Tanganyika, which was ruled by Germany, followed democratic principles but later changed and enjoyed one political party system that hedged on dictatorship. Yet those African countries ruled by France, Belgium, and Portugal were unstable and experienced guerilla wars before they gained their independence. Strange to say, those in power were seen as the enemy of the state, and through their barracks, coups d'état were organized to overthrow their natural governments even before they taught their citizens the meaning of democracy and the rule of law. To many it became the rule of the gun.

It was surely very difficult to push democratic ideals on people or citizens who were 100 percent illiterate and poor. Disease remained atrocious. While the leaders were educated, the masses struggled day and night to put bread on the table. Surprisingly those in power didn't want to be opposed.

It was at this time of independence that the developed nations began a sort of "civil society–driven change." Why? To try to educate the people of the civil society organizations (CSOs) that would not be under the control of government. And in this respect, developed nations made sure that these CSOs were not for moneymaking. They were called "value driven" to change their political perception. Included in the CSOs were nongovernmental organizations (NGOs). It is sad to say that the political parties were not happy with what these groups were doing.

It was Professor Roger Soltau who stated that people who exercise power enjoy it to the hilt and want more and that the ruled to obey—"They exist for the sake of power." Yet one professor B. O. Ukuje, wrote that education develops a person physically, mentally, spiritually, morally, and socially, but the educated leaders hate those they rule and don't want them to enjoy freedom and therefore use the rule of thumb and don't care about their people. As a result, poverty thrives. Diseases like TB and HIV/AIDS now affect millions of Africans.

Be that as it may, what is wrong with Africans? It is only education that is lacking. We have everything via the grace of God. We have oil, gold, diamonds, and other minerals, yet instead of educating our sons and daughters to learn how to enjoy our God-given wealth, we invite the white man! Remember when the first Boers of South Africa arrived? The residents gave them gold in exchange for colored beads!

One aspect of our lives as Africans is that we enjoy wasting time and we love sitting on our laurels, expecting free things. But when the white man introduced CSOs, it was an opportune moment for us to follow the issues of development fast like the nations bordering China that are now ahead of us economically. In addition, we had to follow human rights and hold our leaders accountable when change was needed. Unfortunately we have embraced impunity and corruption.

Perhaps because we abhor reading, as a tool to acquire knowledge, we have failed to acquire three things that are, again, God-given. These are to be able to think rationally and logically and shout when things go wrong. At the same time, we must have the courage to act by demonstrating against oppression the same way it was done in South Africa by Indians during the era of Mahatma Gandhi and later by Nelson Mandela. Unfortunately, without education, changes are impracticable.

Finally, social, political, and economic change can only be realized in Africa through the education of our people. First, though, as the saying goes, "the stomach must be full for the spirit to roam." In this respect, we must have good leaders—but not "benevolent dictators"—who must know how to eradicate poverty. And when resources like oil are discovered, they must be used to raise the standard of living of the people. The people must be educated. Our leaders must pay more attention to agriculture to sustain our own development and provide food sustenance instead of having our crops go to developed nations like China, the majority of Europe, and the USA. We must get food to feed our own people. Isn't it possible that these nations give aid and build infrastructure with strings attached?

Last but not least, Africa must ask all its sons and daughters living in the developed world to come back home and release Africa from the poverty trap as a result of our people's not reading books to discover where the rain began beating us. We must embrace creativity and innovation. We have everything—land, rivers, and equatorial climate. We don't have winters, and a nation like Kenya has its animal heritage—not zoos! The wildlife, rivers, and mountains can make us the "United States of Africa" without wars and genocide!

DISFRANCHISED WOEFUL AFRICA

We were born black.
This is good luck!
Euros were born white.
What they do isn't right.
They've gold, silver, and diamonds.
We too have gold, silver, and diamonds
In their land.
We too have minerals in our land,
Even oil
In our black soil,
Yet they come and steal.
This is against God's will.
But we are fools!
Great fools.
We just watch and smile
With an empty smile,
And they look at us and smile,
But ours is a foolhardy smile,
The asinine smile.
Theirs is a meritorious smile,
Having stolen our property,
Even our liberty.

Why steal our liberty
And give it to us as our property?
Then we pay in the wrong way
Via our natural resources,
Not their resources.
And they've their God-given property,
But Africa is our property,
God-given property.
But with minerals and oil
Deep in bowels of the soil,
They use machines to excavate,
While we enjoy and try to hibernate,
Leaving them to enjoy their spoil.
And they happily drill and steal our oil,
Put it in tankers,
And employ us to drive the tankers.
It's like sending a thief
To catch a thief!
They give us loans,
World Bank loans,
Moving us like puppetry,
And truly we behave like puppetry.
Despite all the education,
We can't think or pay attention!
Woe to Africa,
The disfranchised woeful Africa.

Dr. Joan Ngunnzi

My hope is for justice, for peace, for tolerance, and for acceptance. But mostly, my hope is for love—unconditional.

I am a mother of two—a woman, twenty-two, and a young man, nineteen—both in Jomo Kenyatta University studying public health and computer studies, respectively.

I hold a PhD in education from Kenyatta University, where I specialized in educational communication and technology. I did researched on the sexual abuse of schoolchildren by teachers. I earned a master of arts in disaster management (and I see life itself as a disaster) from the University of Nairobi and a bachelor's degree in English and literature from Moi University. For ten years I served as high school teacher of English and was a principal of Kyaani Girls' Secondary School in Kitui County. I worked at the Teachers Service Commission for fifteen years, resigning in 2015 to take up a new challenge as general manager for education and the Equity Group Foundation, which I quit in 2017 to become minister for gender, children, culture, and social services. I compose and sing. I love laughing and seeing the funny side of life, and I write lots of poems. I have been thinking of writing a book of poetry based on the harrowing narratives I heard about violence against children during my research. I am a philanthropist by DNA too and love swimming and traveling.

I HAVE HEARD

I have heard.
I have heard the public outcry,
A cry against amorous men
Sinking their sickles into babes' virgin lands
And planting seeds of discord.

Learned men of coveted credentials
With their discerning maladaptation to the dangling pieces—
Those imbeciles!
Oblivious of today's human rights
And expanded litigation latitude.
They can only last so long.

DUPED

Duped, dazed, and drowsy
From a slimy stupefying soup,
Sewn together with diligence
To tear down timidity,
Consumed in the comfort of a cozy couch.

She was all over
After all was over.
She lay there unattended,
Unnoticed,
Like cassava in Casablanca.
But for her knee-high Knickerbocker boots
That stood out like an anthill
At Kapiti Plains,
Never would she have been found.

Her client
Figures out his next move
To quieten the raging flood
As the crowd surges on
To confront brutality with naivety.

THE LAST BULLET

He fired.
She fired.
He missed.
She missed.
He fired again
And missed but followed with a club.
So she realized it was war,
No longer a funny game,
Peekaboo.
She would make proper use
Of her last bullet!

STUCK IN KISMAYU

I got stuck in Kismayu.
Not literally,
But
Yes,
I got stuck in Kismayu,
Catching squirrels,
Trying to establish
A multimillion-dollar industry.
Indeed.
A squirrel slaughterhouse
And a
Charcoal chilling chimney.

FIRE FOXES

Next
He beckoned with his googly eyes.
The bear head a bobbly attitude and the bare-knuckles approach
That proved the true enterprise
In disaster.
So each one soldiers on
Through an endless queue,
Clueless,
Clumsy.

"Hell!"
Comes a shout from behind,
A shout from one tired
Of endless lines that circumvent serious solemnity.
He had had enough of sanity
Baked in pig pong.

PICTURE ON THE WALL

There is a picture,
A disturbing picture,
A picture of a child
Desperately crying out for help,
Feeble, faint, forlorn, and fearful,
Groaning, winching, and squealing with pain.
That picture
Hangs on the wall of my heart.
And I must do something
To unhang that picture
This time.

IN THIS LIFE

In this life
I have seen them,
People who merely cover ground. And time.

There are those who see but don't see.
There are those who see but see through.
And others see and only worry
If others have seen.

There are those who hear but don't hear.
There are those who overhear.
And others hear and only worry
If others heard.

There are those who do but don't do.
There are those who do but overdo.
And others only worry
If others did.

But
Whether we see,
Whether we hear,
Whether we do,
We all end up
At the same spot
With those who never bothered
Whatsoever.

POETRY FROM NIGERIA

Ngozi Olivia Osuoha is a Nigerian poet/writer. She earned a graduate degree in estate management with experience in banking and broadcasting. She has published over one hundred poems and articles in over ten countries. Her two longest pieces, one of 355 verses and the other of 560, verses titled *The Transformation Train* and *Letter to My Unborn*, published in Kenya and Canada, respectively, are available from Amazon.com. Her work is featured in over ten international anthologies. She is a passionate African ink who loves her family.

HERDSMANIZATION

In memory of those killed by herdsmen, especially in Benue State, Nigeria

Grazing in cities and highways,
Grazing in schools and farmlands,
Grazing on lives and properties:
Herdsmanization—woe of nomadic farming.

Laying siege against a people,
Waylaying indigenes for animals,
Ambushing citizens for beasts,
Attacking and burning humans:
Herdsmanization—foe of nomadic farming.

They butcher scores
And leave sores.
They burn stores
And destroy chores.
They turn whores
For tiny pores.
Herdsmanization: woe of nomadic farming.

Killing for religion,
Flesh for tradition,
Blood for culture,
Animals for norms,
Cattle for heads,
Cows for gurus,
Grasses for giants,
Fields for future.
Herdsmanization: foe of nomadic farming.

RELIGIOUS BEASTS

Some are magicians
Deceiving the people;
Some are morticians
Embalming the people.

Some are extremists
Fighting with the rod;
Some are terrorists
Killing for their God.

Some are famous,
Well-known by the world;
Some are dangerous,
Not known to the world.

Some are close like friends
All over the place.
They meet at all ends
With different faces.

They have their union,
Even without our knowledge.
They have their communion
Within their college.

Horrors of religion
Amid the fold, divine
Terrors of legion
Among the golden line.

Religious beasts
Spreading tentacles,
Performing miracles,
Crushing obstacles,
Towering pinnacles,
Celebrating their feasts.
In a twinkle, they leave twinkles
That shrink like wrinkles.

POLITICAL MONSTERS

They are the gangsters
In many disciplines,
Cooking the youngsters
To poison their wines.

They are the tricksters
Misguiding the populace
To feed the pranksters
At their own pace.

They are the masters
Playing every card
To suit their plasters
And make it hard.

They are the ill wind
Blowing left, right, front, and back,
Destroying the blind,
Ensuring that they always lack.

They are the undercover,
Wining and dining around,
So that you do not take cover
Until they send you underground.

They are the chameleon
In beautiful colors,
But are the real Napoleon
With a cancerous odor.

Political monsters, the cankerworms
That stir the storm
And trouble our form.
The termite that eats our norm
And destroys our reform.
Political monsters, the beasts after our peace.

CAMPAIGN PROMISES, A BUNCH OF BALDERDASH

The land is green;
In fact, I bring you paradise.
Forget the turmoil and torment.
I am the Messiah and Savior.
Look, I come in peace.
Heaven sent me to you.
Weep no more; wail no more.
I have come. Rejoice,
For your savior is here!
A bunch of balderdash.

I will take you to heaven
And let you dine with God.
You shall become a holy dove
Instead of a wild raven.
I have started the move;
Just give me a nod.
A bunch of balderdash.

I will raise your ancestors
And call forth your unborn.
I will give you security
And grant you amnesty.
I will give you peace
And let your bone grease.
Campaign promises,
A bunch of balderdash.

Jobs shall look for you
And employments break you through.
No more prisons, no more crimes,
No more wars, no more terrors.
I have bargained with natural disasters.
No more earthquakes, no more tsunami.
Never again shall hurricanes rage.
Landslides have been totally silenced.
Wildfires now reside in hell,
And floods have been sent back to the seas.
I have bound them all.
Fear not; worry not:
I have come.

Campaign promises—
A bunch of balderdash.

Look, poverty is dead,
Starvation gone, hate defeated.
Racism is subdued and terrorism done.
Listen, from now, henceforth
All people are equal
Because we all
Were born equal.
No more evil.
Welcome to heaven.
Campaign promises—
A bunch of balderdash.

An open check to woes.
A letter of deceit.
A craft of roguery.
A road to treachery.
Campaign promises.
If you believe them,
Then blame yourself.

THE MAGIC

I do not need a wing to fly.
Neither do I need a plane to travel.
I need no linking park.
Born to fly,
Born to travel,
Born a link,
I am the wind,
I am the air,
I am the breeze.
Harsh or soothing,
Hard or soft,
Wild or mild,
Mean or gentle.
Life, the teacher
Events, the preacher
Life, the bender
Events, the defender.
My piece, my peace.
My ink, my charm.
My aura, the magic.

LETTER TO MANDELA
(They Have Killed Ubuntu)

Things are falling apart.
Homes they vow to thwart.
We are no longer at ease.
Lives they always erase.
It is not the arrow of God
But the wickedness of a god;
They have killed Ubuntu.

You fiercely fought apartheid,
And your destiny untied.
Your long walk to freedom
Was an act of wisdom,
The audacity of hope
Inspired in order to cope.
They just killed Ubuntu.

Frying people like potato
May cause nightfall in Soweto.
The message of Mandela
Preaches no violence for Madiba.
The dream of your fathers
Contributed to your prison diary.
Where then is Ubuntu?

There was a country

With half a yellow sun
Almost wiped away by the gun,
By an adverse effrontery.
A victim of circumstance
Searching for greener pastures,
Ubuntu is murdered.

Papa Africa, call them to order.
Enough is enough.

#Killing of strangers is un-African

BLOODLAND

Dear ECOWAS,
We pray in church;
They prey with charm.

Dear African Union,
We shout with pen;
They shoot with gun.

Dear European Union,
We go to farm;
They do us harm.

Dear United Nations,
We have become rodents;
They kill us like bush meats.

Dear Amnesty International,
We live in bondage;
They go on rampage.

Dear world,
Your map may erase us soon,
The rivers of Africa,
If you count Niger.
You may forget Benue.

There is a coup by cattlecracy,
The overthrow of humankind by namacracy.
There is a reign of grazingcracy,
The colonization by nomads.
There is an overflow of blood,
The rulership of herdsmencracy.

Dear world,
Lo, we drown in bloodland.
These heavenly breeds send us to hell;
Is your silence a consent?
For now is the end of time.

IF WE ALL WERE CATTLE

If we all were cattle,
Herdsmen would not bear arms.

If we all were herdsmen,
Cattle would not graze harms.

If we all bore arms,
Cattle would not raze farms.

If we all grew farms,
Cattle would not blow charms.

If we all were scams,
Cattle would have no qualms.

If our past were cattle
And our present battle,
Then our future is rattle.

This sacred cow
Against a scapegoat.
Remember, a vow
Can disarm any boat
And waste its oat
By merely asking how.

If we all were herdsmen,
If we all were cattle,
If we all were scams,
If we all had qualms,
If we all grazed harms,
If we all blew charms,
If we all bore arms,
If we all fought a battle,
If we this snake rattle,
Then our past,
Our present,
And our future,
All, would be a flood of muddy blood.

PUNCTURED NATURE

I am Mother Nature.
You widen my exposure.
Listen now, dear earth.
Listen; hear my breath.
I have been punctured
And even captured.
I am falsely pregnant
Courtesy of chemicals,
Protruding tummy balloon,
Total womb vacancy.
Wild human radicals
Finally breeding a baboon.
I am the breast.
I cannot suckle again.
My milk is sour.
I am no longer fit for feast,
Because I am in pain.
So they turn to flour.
That is not the least.
I am the sacred breast.
For breakthrough
They puncture my walls,
Cut me through,
And plant their balls.

I am the fetus.
They flush me with drugs
So they can focus
And maintain their hugs
With a deceitful kiss,
Yet they dare not hiss.
I am the buttocks.
They pierce me from the top,
Insert heavy blocks.
There, they never stop.
They put in me a wedge
And build a round hedge.
I am the eye.
Normally, I am black.
Now, me they dye,
Send me to the back
As though I am useless.
Yet, it is not their success.
I am the skin.
Natural, I am beautiful,
But they wash me thin,
So sometimes I look fearful.
Black, white, green, blue;
I even gum like glue.
I am the ozone layer.
They pump gas into me,
Wail for climate change,
Chant, "It is strange,"

Turn a soothsayer,
And say I sting like bee.
I am the land.
They bind my hand,
Mine coal, and drill oil;
So they foil, soil, and boil.
Because they torment me,
And I cannot flee.
I am the ocean,
My own musician.
I make each piece,
And it gives me peace.
Wave, storm, tempest;
I revenge against my rest.
I am the wild animal
They claim to tame,
Even when they are carnal
Just for their fame.
When nature gets me angry,
I devour.

POOR GOD

He floats no political party.
He is not a presidential candidate.
He has no running mate,
Never graduated from any college.
Has no account with a Swiss bank.
Not a drug baron,
And runs no brothels.

He has no religion.
Not a suicide bomber,
Never a racist,
Not a Hollywood actor,
Not a WWE superstar,
Not a crazy hip-hop artist,
Not a world footballer.

Too shy to be seen,
Too calm to be heard,
Too reserved to be noticed.
Poor God, no investment.
No wife, no children.
Poor God; poor heart,
Depressed, sad, and troubled.

Poor God, I really pity you.
I am just wondering.

CRUSADERS OF EVIL

Dear mother giant
Who dwarfeth thee,
Dear dwarf father
Who giantest thee,
That ye callest thyself such.
Thou wag. Why waggest thou?
Why draggest thou thy bag like a rag.
Thou nag. Why sag thy tag?
Hast thou been cursed?
Or art thou a statue, so shameless?
Dear mother giant,
O ye father dwarf,
Thou mean crossbreed, hybrid.
Thou realest fool,
Perching and picking like pigeon.
The crusading masquerade
Parading in barricade
Across the blockade
Of unknown and unborn multitude,
Wait, for time cometh fast.

AGES OF WAR

Ages of war
Shattering our wages,
Dragging us to the edges,
And bruising our hedges.

Ages of pain
Boiling the rain,
Heating our stain,
And fading our gain.

Ages of fears
Flowing like tears,
Pumping our rears,
And scorching our wears.

Ages of sorrow
Selling tomorrow,
Buying a hollow,
And living on what is borrowed.

Ages of violence
Clamping on pretense,
Leaning on negligence,
And lacking sense.

Ages of turmoil
Losing the oil,
Loving the toil,
Buried in the soil.

Ages of oppression
Hanging on suppression
Without suggestion
And busy with destruction.

Ages of wickedness
Flagged by crookedness.
Ages of darkness
Ruined by backwardness.

Ages of lust
Tasting the dust.
Nothing is just—
All a terrible must.

Ages of torture
Without a lecture,
Finding no gesture
And dying in pressure.

Ages of death.
No air, no breath.
Ages at length.
No cure, no strength.

Ages of war,
Bombs, and missiles.
Ages of war.
Children melting like tiles.

Ages, O ages.
War, O war.

Etim Bassey Onyam, hails from Cross River State, Nigeria. He has many Golden Awards in poetry competitions to his credit. He is currently a project student of English and political science in the College of Education, Afaha Nsit, Nigeria.

Etim Onyam is a onetime senator representing the National Association of English and Literary Studies (NASELS) in the student union government senate, and also a onetime deputy speaker for NASELS, Nigeria.

Etim Onyam is the founder of HAPSS (Home of African Poetry and Splendid Stories), which has inspired many poets.

THE UNTRODDEN PATHS OF AFRICA

I have wandered from the grassland of the savanna
To the great mountains of the north;
From the shores of the Atlantic
To the thick forests of the mangrove;
And now here I stand,
At the point where multiple paths meet.

I have seen paths,
Paths with worn-out edges from repeated treadings,
Paths so wide and congested with egregious failures,
Paths leading to repeated and cyclical endings,
Entrapping Mother Africa in a hideous quagmire and perdition.

I have seen paths that lead to selfishness and knavery,
With corruption and looting as auxiliary routes
I mean paths that empty into ethnicity and nepotism,
Whose footprints are hunger and penury …
Paths whose infectious dusts
Blind excellence and meritocracy
And blindly crowning mediocrity.

Beyond these paths lie the untrodden paths of Africa:
Paths very bushy and narrow with enduring lengths,
Paths at whose entryways lie dry bones,
The forgotten and unmourned bones of those who dared to travel by them
With their names boldly inscribed on golden tablets.

They are the untrodden paths of Africa:
Paths with miraging thongs and sharp stumps,
Paths that lead to mutual peace and harmony;
They are the empty paths of true unity in diversity
And paths that empty into the emancipation of the African mine
From the enduring chains of imperialism and neocolonialism!

In the core of Africa,
The untrodden paths remain the paths to true accountability and transparency,
Paths leading to true democracy and rule of law,
The paths to equitable distribution of the common wealth.
They are the paths that none wishes to wander onto.

I have seen paths,
Paths that countless rulers have promised to lead us onto,
The paths to the shores of better education for all,
Paths to potable water and stable power supply for all,
Paths that seek to balance the inequality between the rich and the poor,
The governors and the governed.

Who shall lead the adventure to these paths?
The paths to which the nationalists only opened the ways,
Hoping this posterity would do the undone …
Arise, O ye budding compatriots of Africa,
For these paths must be explored
To salvage this sinking continent!

AFRICA, SPEAK!

O Africa, mother of the black race,
Thou have been the best mother ever,
But now thy children stray from thy witty counsel.

I beseech you to rise
From thy momentary nap,
Tell our forebears of their straying offspring:

Tell Nkrumah, Macauley, and Madiba
That greed now rules their lands.
Tell them the people they emancipated
Have been "rebundled" into imperialism.

Tell them the resources
They fought to preserve
Have been buried in greedy pockets,
Perpetually enriching the economy of their imperial lords.

Tell them, among other things,
That the rulers are now glued to political thrones like Evo-Stik.
Whisper to Crowther
That in the cathedral planted in place of thy ancient norms,
The clerics now charge our pockets out,
Coded in the trending cantata
Of seed sowing.

Speak of the Arabic voices
Roaming our lands in terror.
Speak of the black skin now traded for white
Through concocted ointments.

Tell Cheb Hasni and Lounès Matoub,
Dube, Fela, and Brenda Fassie,
That music has been buried
Into lustful and themeless voices.

Tell the great farmers
That their lands now lie long fallowed and abandoned
In pursuit of oil, the black gold,
While starvation now raids the lands.

Forget not to tell Achebe
That in the giant of Africa,
Formalism and lustful entertainments have overshadowed
Pragmatic literary writings.
Tell him of the high cost to be lettered,
Of our inks running dry,
And of our exhausted leaves.

Tell him we now write on sands
To be trodden by the feet of men.
Remember also to tell Madiba
That wars and pestilence
Have eaten up the African peace.

And when you have the message,
As I have charged thee to deliver,
Arise and reclaim thy lost glory,
For you shall be great!

Nseobong Edem hails from Akwa Ibom State, Nigeria. He's an award-winning poet and has won many international-based awards in e-poetry competitions, including Golden Prize in a Seven Nations contest and the Peter Benjamin Award for the Poetic World Cup contest, season one. He is currently a project student of English and political science in the College of Education, Afaha Nsit, Nigeria. Nseobong Edem is also a onetime press secretary for the student union government senate, and chapter secretary general in NASELS, Nigeria, and currently he is the financial secretary of Counseling Association Students of Nigeria. He is a poet of high caliber and is secretary of HAPSS (Home of African Poetry and Splendid Stories).

Nseobong Edem believes in his own success through determination and dedication. He is ambitious, self-made, and workaholic.

THE HARD WAY

You were brought abroad
from the tree of undiluted knowledge,
And like a child, you sucked the milk of palatability,
well seasoned with sugariness.
You were fed like a prince and not a pauper.

And your words became the amala,
well seasoned with spices
always ready to be consumed.

But you've watered the system
and the taste.
You've messed with nonattention.
I sat on the bare floor to recite the ABCs,
And the paths were covered by your created seas.
But your sons have eaten the fried rice overseas.

Yes, I've eaten the bread of life,
and I'm so full of that life.
And I've yielded the many fruits
like the seasonal mango fruits
To drop not too many, but all!

I am a poet
who is yet to duet
with my coined words.
I've put life in the wire you wired with no current!
The woman on the street,
yes, I put her in a home you denied her.
The hunger you created.
I made everything bountiful to many.

Mr. Politicking,
I shall split words on your face
and leave you with Hausa facial marks
and drop the feces on tango.
Then I shall challenge your sons to intellectual fist, not a fight,
and to them prove my might,
Provide that truly, I learned this the hard way!

HOW, BROTHER?

I come not to sing songs of praise,
For there's no sycophancy weaved in this piece written in piss.
I come not to beat drums of turpitude,
For there's no evil in my attitude.

How do you bear the brooms of evil
And umbrellas of unchanged devils,
To and fro in the heart of the city,
Muddling our ears, when we are in need of your pity?
How?

Is it to you fun?
When from Etim Ekpo, to Ikot Ekpene, to Ukanafun,
Lives are hushed,
With symbols of no noble cause,
As their blood and flesh wash and litter the land with curses?
Tufiakwa to you!

O how do you sleep in your hilltop mansion,
With so much of 2019 passion
When our mothers run with bare feet,
In a moment covering many feet,
Fleeing their paradise and comfort zone,
Seeking refuge of refuge as refugees in different zones?

Brother! Say to me how you eat
When many are butchered;
With a fainter's fan and pan, their flesh fried!
How, brother?

They're victims of their own hybrids!
Brother turned slayer of brother for brotherhood!
Posterity will never forgive you, Brother! *Uncle Mark!*
I am meticulous about the past,
Our humble and little beginnings,
The days of us struggling for a bowl of food,
Eating like running a marathon race,
Cursing and patting each other in a friendly manner.

But today you build fences as tall as iroko trees,
Demarcating the lines of our ties,
With Beware of Dog placed permanently on your walls,
Which is a lion that roars.

You became exorbitantly rich
And so out of my reach.
Access to you became more expensive than my total income,
With your armed men pounding and slapping me each time I come.

Uncle Mark,
I am here,
Where once I stood to bid farewell to Aso Rock,
But where this time I stand
To bid you an end!

BARBARIAN

I am here to question your stupidity,
Which to you, is wisdom.
I am here to stare at your abnormality,
Which to us—we would've been safe with a condom!
But you were allowed to grow.
And with brimstone, you were nurtured,
Turning you into fire that consumed.

From which tree of knowledge did you eat
That has made you this barbaric?
O which book did you pass from
That has made you a barbarian?
Tell me! What turned you into a vulture,
Which on flesh you feast, so uncultured?

I opened the window
To let the scent of blood out of the tunnel.
Shoving the ashes of humans, not sheep, into buckets,
Which you offered as burnt sacrifice
To marry more virgins in the afterlife.
The after: that afterlife!

Today, everything ticks away,
Never minding the essence of time.
Spacing and the return of frail memories
Has crushed my very innards.

My eyes have traveled in pain;
My ears have heard the echo of misery and hurt;
And in horror, I've screamed,
Opening my veins to bleed out words.

If I could go back to the warmth of her womb,
I wouldn't be here to see so many tombs
Or live in the woods of death.
Please, someone take me back to Mama …

WE'RE ALL GUILTY

Sprinkle me not the waters from that broom.
For in the spirit of the broom,
You came promising a boom.

O play me a melodious tune of art.
To dance and naked the thoughts in my heart
That have been locked in my den,
Never been inked with pen.

Tell the lording lord who lords over my rights
That we're all guilty of these acts.
Tell the man who sits in judgment against me
That we're all guilty of the acts he's accused of.

Have you not heard
That the difference between 8:30 and 11:30 is African?
That is as black as my skin.

As the number doubles,
Waiting at your table,
On tiptoe, you jetted in,
Walking majestically like the queen of Ikorodu,
Chewing gum like a shameless goat
That eats leaves at a moment's notice.
To you, an apology is expensive
And need not be wasted.

With your lording voice, you command with signs
After an hour;
You call for chicken lap,
Washing it down with Coke, while we salivate in anguish.
You jump from one terrain to the other, keeping us in the dark.
Then for the day you close, for the government is ours.
Don't kill yourself!

You stopped at the vendor's place,
Listening to the learned talking about leadership;
You jump into it like a lizard.
I have adjusted my glasses to mirror you well.

At month's end,
Expect no more,
For the man to pay will come to the office in a while.
Criticize no more,
For we're all guilty of ineffectiveness.

FAREWELL SONG

'Tis not an ode.
For to what shall it be addressed as ode?
'Tis not a dance of madness,
For which style shall best suit this forlornness?
But it's just a grief-stricken song
That craves no rapping of the gong
On the starved lips drowned in the sea of grief.

No bridge shall beckon for us to cross over our integrity
Nor shall our temple lose its innocence.
For this sweet venom can't be sucked out.
Shall we not spend days
Picking at the fibers of our sweaters
With this farewell song on our lips?

Who will watch a fuel truck capsize into gallop
With a screeching sound and turned brothers' faces, the tires facing up,
Brushing many with screams and cries of pain
As they rain the ocean of their tears,
Penetrating virgin heart temples with fears?
Firelights turn all to ashes
Like offered burnt sacrifice,
For the man to fix the road
Has built fences like iroko, housing the wealth,

Without joining this farewell song.

Who with a stone heart
Will watch a pregnant mother dissolve in her arms
Like a cube of ice on a lad's palms?
Her sparkling eyes shot beneath closed eyelids,
With no one to dip hands beneath in a quest to save,
For the doctors are on strike
Without singing this farewell song.

Who among us will not feel a happy rage and sensuous muttered joy
To watch an ailing sister's weeping lips
In agonizing, joyous pain and with open ocean eyes,
Like the rising of the dark sun, breathing her last,
Begging to be buried adrift,
Sleeping with no tomorrow,
For there are no drugs?
The man who was to buy the drugs
Has sent his sons abroad to sniff hard drugs
Without tuning aloud this farewell song.

Who'll watch our father's emaciated bones
Shivering in torn and shrunken clothes at the ministry's gate
With placards not of hate,
Begging to be paid a pension?
Like flies, they drop one by one, waiting for the payday,
And there are names wiped off
Without hymning this farewell song.

At the height of hunger and starvation,
Situated at the very fiber of your being,
Please tune this farewell song.
At the height of insecurity and bloodbath,
With your brother's pool of blood like a bath on the path,

Please echo this farewell song!
And let the stars of the earth give o'er ear to bleeding hearts!
O let the sun burn our sumptuous words into hearts
And carry on her body our burden to Aso Rock,
Not of ages, but house of cemetery-like rock.

Let them again come with trucks of *maggi*, rice, and wrappers
To intoxicate and rob us again
For their selfish gain!
But on our crumbled pages and our thin lips,
Beneath the thousands of broken prayer beads,
They shall mete on us this farewell song!

If ever you grow curious for light and standard education,
Don't refrain from yelling loud.
If ever you deserve fair treatment, the same as the elite class,
Please echo this farewell song.
And let it in. It brings freedom!
For this farewell song is one of freedom
To save Africa.

SAVE AFRICA FROM THAT MAN

I lay on my bed as the bed box boxed my body
In my microwaved room with no fan to fan the fannable out of my body!
I only heard of 24/7 electricity when I came to your mansion.
As I read the things that were dear me in my portion,
On the pages I saw you epitomizing misconduct.

Tell the man
In hotel rooms who wets every pot,
Slithering his nylon tongue slowly,
To and fro, on the insides of many honeypots,
Hoping to find the pathway that leads him to heaven,
Using his fingers to run high notes on snake-hipped bodies,
His balls balling like the beating of bongo drums,
With them giving silent screams that silence my eardrums.
But he's from Oga!
Please, when you see him,
Tell him that Africa needs to be saved.

Please tell the man
Who receives standing ovation
At every occasion,
Perceived to be of noble character
But who mops the treasury dry

With a mop greater than the mops of the moppers when mopping,
Robbing me of light, standard education, and a job.
Yet he pours his lies down my throat,
Infecting my lungs with lies that are indigestible,
Which later turn to lice in my wounds,
Licking, as I in painful pleasure smile.
When you see him,
Tell him that Africa needs to be saved!

Tell the man—
An attorney, that man!—
Sitting on judgment of me
To rob me of my land and in emptiness leave me,
For I do not have a brown branded envelope to offer …
Just tell him
Africa needs to be saved.

Please tell the man
Who bequeathed everything
To his brothers, sisters, and uncles,
As I in the streets wander to no destination
With chopped certificate, chopped by rats—
Please, when you see him,
Tell him that Africa needs to be saved!

SICK SINKING SHIP

O sinking ship
On a free fall,
When will you hit the bottom coil?

Sick of blood!
Did the blood of Ken Saro-Wiwa 'n' others
Not appease your thirst for blood?
Or has the Benue pool of blood
Not fed your bowl to the brim?

Sick of wealth!
Has the pilfering not filled your star pockets?
Or did the golden snake not make it to your shrine
With filled mouth of surplus wealth?

Sick of girls!
Did the Chibok girls
Not pass the virginity test;
To hush your urge?

Sick of abuse!
Has the named dog killed and eaten,
Not caressing your intestine
Or belonging to Za Ola room,

Not solved the mathematics of doom?
Did the idle youth not trek
From Makurdi to Aso Rock to hail hell?
Dino Melaye proved that Usain Bolt traced on armless;
But tortoises crawl on Benue slayers endlessly!

We all saw hailed crusader and activist,
Now wailing wailer for fighting intellectual fist!

Tell Sola Owonibi
That the homeless are hopeless and injected with fear.
Tell Ola Rotimi
That the gods of Britain are blamed
For this failed marriage like the lame.
Ask Chimamanda Adichie
When half of the yellow sun will turn full
To brighten our murky path.
Plead with Ayi Armah
To release the beautiful ones,
To extricate us!

O sinking ship
And sickening sick!
Can the sick seek to heal the sick?
Hit the bottom at once, and start afresh;
Or die a cold death with bleeding and torn flesh!

HERE'S NOT MY HOME

When a morning mass
Is turned to a burial ceremony en masse,
Please let the stars twinkle in murkiness
And usher me into a reposing home,
For here is not my home!

When children are but infected chicken
That need be slaughtered in winter and broken,
Please let the fluttering dove
Tendering me with wings to fly away
And assemble my home in a desert in a land far away,
For here is not my home
But cemetery to my kind.

When riding a bicycle,
Outdo the broom that sprinkles
Chains, like change.
Let the idle youths rise
Like the sunrise
And right it with PVC,
For here is not our home!

BROTHER'S BLADE

I will wear the green and white colors
And march in a prideful parade like the sailors.
I will rhythmically beat the canister
And sing songs of praise like the choristers.
But when the sun sets for the infantry,
I shall take a sad bow for this, my country.

So you feel you know how I feel?
Because I say I am proudly filled?

Get off the hook!
And take that golden olden book
That's covered with dust with the name Nigeria.
Be sure it's Nigeria and not Liberia.
Then breathe some life into it!
Make it sit as you will like it,
Then take this message like question:
Ask, but never question!

I live in a country
Where men sit under the mango tree
As the moon shines to its fullness.
They sway in a circle for happiness,
Taking turns in telling moonlight stories.

Then another sits sharpening the blunt machete, charging the batteries,
Not to farm but to do barbaric things.
He takes it to the circle,
Then cuts them like plants and willow,
Undressing skeletons and leaving them bare.
And with enthusiasm, he giggles while cleaning the red wet stains.
(For how long shall you close your eyes and watch?)

I live in a country where education is a sin,
Turning these places into killing scenes.
The schoolgirls kidnapped in trucks on a daily basis,
Right through the noses of these shameless officers' faces.
Then the government calls for a party,
Dining and dancing together in this party,
As they do the billion bargain
For fiasco selfish gain
To keep them in perpetual darkness
And then brainwash girls with religion.
(How long shall you watch your ship sink?)

I live in a country
Where like the Igbo, visitors down the kegs of wine.
Men sit to feed the barrels of guns,
To hunt not animals but fellow men for fun!
Then at the market, they set their digger,
Freeing the unclad metals by a pull of the trigger.
After the hot metals dart randomly,
A total silence is heard,
Followed by screams of horror, pain, and death.
Then as one starts to count—
1 ... 2 ... 3 and counting—
Children shout, "*Mama!*"
And like the dogs, they're made to rest.
(For how long shall your heart be made to bleed?)

Please, when you see these men,
Run as far as your legs can carry you!
Run before you're used to score another political goal.
Run and never turn back!
Run and run!
But when your legs fail to carry you,
Or when you reach the walls
And you're still being pushed and pinned to the walls,
Turn and die not a cowardly but a noble death.
Down as many as you can,
Then rest on your brother's blade!

Chidi Nwosu is a Nigerian entrepreneur, poet, writer, and social and political commentator. His poems have been published in several anthologies and journals all over the world.

ONE DAY

one day
after the vultures
had picked clean
the cadavers
and the only memories left
are seas of white bones,
we shall remember
the peace we should've
sown decades ago.
one day
after the tears
of widows dry up
and left are furrows
of sorrow on their faces,
we shall remember
the peace pipe
we refused to smoke.
one day
after the famine
precipitated by wars
and lawlessness,
we shall remember
the rule of law
we had forsaken.

one day
after all the youths
are gone,
and left are bent men
and women
and the chasms
of bygone eras,
we shall remember
how we ate all our produce
before harvest.
one day
after the country
is balkanized,
each will be left holding
a fragile piece,
a peace worthless.

GATHERING STORMS

haunting are the giggles
of hyenas,
foreboding the songs
of owls.
macabre, the jubilating
dances of the vultures.
they're gathering
like the storms
for the next elections.
their avalanches are rolling
tiny flakes upon
tiny flakes.
we the people
wait as we're used to
to welcome it with crushed
bones.

TO TALK IS TO DIE

freedom is dead.
to talk is to die.
to cry against
the itch on our scrotums
is death.
our hands cuffed,
our mouths locked,
our eyes folded,
our feet chained.
even freedom to groan
under our heavy yokes
denied.
onward, like captives
of ISIS,
we are marching silently
to the guillotines.

Francis Annagu lives in Southern Kaduna, Nigeria, where he is referred to as Southern Kaduna's most prominent poetic voice. He has had quite a lot of poems featured in *Libations for Nigeria Anthology, Dead Snakes, London Grip New Poetry, The Unbroken Smile, Potomac Journal, Crannog Magazine,* and elsewhere. A rights activist and a member of Young African Leaders Initiative, he studied political science at Kaduna State University.

OUR LAND IN A DESERT TROUGH

Our land potted in the scorched
trough of a little desert pond,
cracked in the ravaging sun;
a treasury of coins and contracts,
but the poor have no basket to
harvest fallow plots of niggard
wheat, while the wealthy at
round tables sit for cowry shells,
more in a rowdy toast for their iron
greed.

Our famished land drank a lot
of wine from the vulture's pot
of greed, ever since the masses
trooped the parliament gates,
horrified and exhausted with the
colony of oats and omelets,
with urchins on a long trek
from the untended rice paddies.

The poor are hungry since their
corn farms have no drizzle to

grow grains in the harmattan,
and when the east wind blows,
death will make a harvest of
the feeble people of ridicule,
dancing tearfully like a baobab,
reciting mumbles of a mocking
bird, the razzled cries heard.
But a sheriff passed among the
vultures, stealing our trinket boxes.

At night the hoots of owls are
in chorus with the tidal grouse of
workers' unions against inflation,
and the shortage of petro-naira that
stunted the economy as the rampages
in the quarter moved toward
succor over suffering, and every
step we take, is for the crack of dawn.

Pounding boots announce the rancors
in the overblowing grime of turbulence
and the heat that harbors our cricks, but
our leaders are merry behind electric gates,
turning away their transient smiles from
the tumults of our land that drink
a lot of wine from the vulture's pot of greed.

AFRICA (A CHILD)

Awake, dark soul rebuked
on the day of Nkrumah's liberation.

Awake from the hammering boots
of the West.
O Africa awake, child,
you banished Zambezi child.

Hidden within the tracks of slavery
and the forbidden limits of your
mother's call.

Child, awake from this trivial prison
and see
the sore bleeding from your father's wound.

As they bound him to incendiary chains,
the cowboys of dubious desires
founded the Suez of running treasures.

Remember your mother's call
from the tongue of pure love awakening.

SONG OF BUSI MHLONGO

Day dawned, dabbed
sensually round the ferret sun,
revealing Africa's luminous hills,
coupling soul and passion
plunged in a soulful voice,
crackling with many pods of freedom
for the next season of blooming democracy
far away from apartheid
and the desert of vexation.

Dimples of your hills
crisp and colored.
Rwanda's genocide blades.
Africa.

One who knows the
archaeology of beauty
values the emeraldry of your name,
your translucent skin,
complexion undiluted,
as foliates of the AU tree,
as totemic calendar of royalty.

From the names of your
reverberating songs,
hear the birds crooning
through horizons, through rainbows,
across ever-lush grasslands
feeding the Wolof boy's herd,
the abundance of evergreen grasslands.

Our spirits
are high up, Africa,
lettered in brilliant colonnade
of your venerated names, with countless stars aglow beyond
Niamey's city
of flying bullets.

ELEPHANT

Our land remains, climbing up
the plastic tree of wealth
for its penchant love of golden fruits.

So we sit daily under the giant oak
to design the crumbled structures of
his feet on the slippery back of the
banana tree, scorning an elephant
plunking its neck with overgreased
palms up to the peak of a branch.

But our eyes have not seen a mere
haunt in midday that overran
the tall, slippery banana tree.

As he climbed up, we discovered our
eyes were engulfed by the awesome and
intriguing show when the mighty
one in a ravenous sound fell
on sharp and stubborn grasses.

Udekwe Chikadibia is a Nigerian writer and poet from the Igbo-Igala-speaking eastern region, Igga in Uzo-Uwani LGA, Enugu State. He is currently studying English language and literature (BEd) at Nwafor Orizu College of Education in affiliation with the University of Nigeria Nsukka. He is a poetry lover and an ardent student of literature. He is an unpublished but an award-winning poet. He is a member of Poets in Nigeria (PIN) and the National Association of Students of English and Literary Studies (NASELS).

TRAGIC

She was decapitated
After the hot hurting rape
From the three able-bodied youths
Of hopelessness and incurable curses.
Breasts were taken away coercively,
G-spot was left bloody, and
Red waters flooded out furiously
Here and there.
Legs and their sisters were taken too.
It was a total amputation.
This was done to a mother of three
In a nearby community,
Who went to the farm to farm
What her children would eat,
For her husband had gone to greet the grave,
Which called him untimely.
This is nothing but tragic!

I WAS MADE TO BELIEVE

I was made to believe
that gerontocracy is the best crazy,
the best system that would term youths lazy.
I was made to believe this right from my cradle.

I was made to believe
that our leaders are werewolves,
that I have to believe strongly that they're our woes.
I was made to believe this right from my infancy.

I was made to believe
that the lazy youths are the leaders of blind tomorrow,
but the youths I am seeing now are in sweet sorrow.

I was made to believe this hook, line, and sinker.
Let me stop here, for a word is enough …
and my beliefs are mammoth.
I do not want them to wriggle out like maggots.
But dear listener, be informed that we practice gerontocracy,
and our leaders are not wane werewolves,
and the lazy youths are the leaders of blind tomorrow.

April 21, 2018

Nosar Philips (Pentooth) is a business-minded person who craves joy in writing. He hails from Nigeria, Africa.

UNTITLED (ENIYAN)

Lost in lust,
Confused in a person's look,
Sworn to decide by the sword swipe.
It's so sad. I feel bad,
For my dreams shattered
All to powder by my hatred.
But my son, I see the Ojos pleading for years.
It is extremely hard
To open the lock of my heart
After your sister was killed.
How do I believe the lies,
The unholy worship of Eniyan?
Even though I miss their bliss,
Affection, and sacrificial attention,
Darkness awakes, and the sun dies.
Eniyan!
Who came to plead *yeye*'s milk.
Their treachery haunts them
Behind their dream windows.
Frivolous and obnoxious dreams.
Eniyan is cruel!
They are human chicks.
They shall see me when the sun beholds their eyes on the day of the coming.

I wonder how the Christian God has mercy on them.
Eniyan.
Okay. I will be brave and forgiving, for I cannot choose to forever weep.
But as I send you to Eniyan
Year after year,
Tell them about my anger,
Anger enough to boil the whole marine world.
I will be happy.
Let them nary do evil,
For I know,
Eniyan is cruel.

UNTITLED (AMOPE)

The scariest disguise I could wear.
The picture of a beast that children saw at Erie Junction.
On the surface I am happy.
But I had something pursuing me.
I am quite the masquerade man.
I'm the jolly friend, smiling.
Native chalk-sharing monster.
Behind this mask, a ruse.
Everybody here thinks I'm perfect.
They can't look inside.
Soberness would break me soon,
Me, a masquerade man.
Our blessings and wealth is a heresy.
Beneath the mask, a painted face;
Our costumes now our second skin.
We pay the price to act like gods.
Gin is my sacrifice.
Barren women see us as Priapus.
And at Ekpenede I saw Amope.
Following her was imperative. Amope, all the way from Ile Nfe,
I must follow you to your land.

David Chukwudi Njoku

"I am a Nigerian poet and writer. I am also a faith preacher, a lover of poetry, and a songwriter. My utmost desire is to make a positive impact on the world with God's Word and poetry.

"My education qualification: I studied banking and finance at the Polytechnic, Birnin Kebbi Nd, in 2003. My book titled *Pick Up That Pen* was published by Spectrum House, UK, in 2018. My poetry has appeared in the following anthologies: *Harmony* (2017), *Our Poetry Archive* (2013), *Bonjour Février* (2018), and *World Institute for Peace* (2018). I won first place in the Poetry Wall competition, 2018; was runner-up of the 2018 Colors of Life contest, and received recognition for an outstanding performance on International Women's Day. My hobbies include writing, reading, and doing research. Being a member of the clergy has helped me to churn mysteries in the world of poetry."

SAVE AFRICA: THE PREACHER BLEEDS

Hey,
You there,
I'm here
With the words of the Creator
To bring you salvation from the scripture.
My preaching is against
The rulers of injustice,
The killers of destinies,
The parasitic flu,
The jungle justice,
The chameleon in power
That dashes the hope of the citizens.
Can I get an amen?

Hey,
You there,
I mean here,
I'm now on stage
As the preaching sage
With another page
To speak against
Nepotism,

Racism,
Tribalism,
The emerging wars
Right here in Africa.
The case of Syria
Is disheartening,
Damaging,
So cancerous.
Let's stop the civil wars
Within nations.

Let's not wait for the full moon
When the werewolves
Would take form.
Let's get the oak
And take away their cloak.

Let's wake up, friends.
Pick up your pen again.
Don't just write or say;
Live what you write and say.
Don't be ashamed again.

"Preach, Preacher," they chorused.

See how they've enmeshed us
Deep into poverty,
Slavery even in our land,
Our nativity sold
For a morsel of bread?
I stand against these chameleons' integrity.

What's in democracy?
Are we in democracy?

Or family-cracy?
Or dementia-cracy?

Pain I be as I preach.
Preach I not because of meat,
Not even because of fame
Nor the gains of fame.
But I preach to make a change
In the game of fame.

Now say I to you,
Arise,
Arise.
Be not afraid.
Let's knit together
And sound the doctrine of the Creator
To stop these barbaric
Carnivorous mammals.

Arise and pick up.
Pick up your pen
Against these poisonous asps.
Their viper's tongues shall we
Slay, slaying it by picking up
Our pen to swallow their darkness
With light from our pen.

WE ARE NOT PRISONERS

We're not prisoners,
No, never are we,
But we own the land together.
Why be prisoners
In our own land?

We're not slaves,
No, never are we,
But we share together
The stakes of resources.
Why treat us like slaves?

We're now sojourners
In our native lands.
Why do the leaders
Take the spoils
That belong to us all?
We're not prisoners.

It is a shame
That our leaders
Are our killers
Who have fellowship
With dictatorship.
We're not prisoners.

Who shall save Africa?
Who shall protect Africa?
We need a savior, now,
To come out from this prison.

AWAY WITH THE DEAD

Away with the dead.
They stink.
They're perverse,
Full of treachery.
Away with the dead

How come they lead
When they're dead?
How bewitched we are,
Living with the dead.
Away with the dead.

Power in the hands of the dead
Is an otiose experiment.
Ouch! It is like fish on dry land.
Away with the dead.

This song of the dead
Must not awake.
It must remain dead.
Away with the dead.

Let's murder the ossified wand of politics.
Civil war is cancerous,
For limpness and miscarriage
Will be our bane of damage.

Arise, arise. Sleep no more.
Away with the dead!

Away with marriage of convenience.
Away with these frozen frosty elements
Without regard for human lives.
Away with the dead.

Pray we for living,
A true living crop of leaders
Who are alive
To stop the ranting of the dead.
Away with the dead.

Nwankwo Christian is a Nigerian poet. Since he was a child, art has been his hobby, and his special interest in poetry grew in high school as he read many poetry books and articles. In 2010 he wrote his first poem, titled "Birds of Many Colors." Since that time, he has been greatly active in the poetry world, having featured in many local and international anthologies.

I AM A BLACK, AN AFRICAN AMERICAN

I am the voice crying for your help.
I am the one stolen from my father's land.
I am the one your whipper bent like wood.
I am the one you segregated and abandoned.
I am your beggar and the black awareness.
I am the color you look upon like something thrown away.
I am the one whose children you killed.
I am the river you worked so hard to sand-fill.
I am the crime you love so much to commit.
I am the face you declared null and void.
I am the slave whose sweat and blood built your nation.
I am the life you cut short to increase your gain.
I am the one you saw and became a racist.
I am the Negro you said is unmatched to you.
I am the one they gave freedom to but still imprisoned.
I am a black, an African American.

Ayomide Samuel is a student from Nigeria.

MAGNIFICENT IMAGE

Heroes on the battlefield
Of motherhood, a superb image
Of God's dexterity,
She is a god after God's heart.
Through her, nations build strength,
And towers wax strong and tall.

In her heart she carries
Her child more than her arm.
Fearless, courageous, and
Determined, she is in her field.
With tears, blood, a yell, and a smile,
She fights her battle
To see her seed yielding
Sweet fruit.

For the love of her fruits,
She renders her life with no penny,
Like that of a sheep in the hand
Of its skin shaver.
Her precious gold and pride
She sows to build her nation
Strong and mighty.

In stormy and calm seas,
She sails her boat
Just to get to her shore.
Without any glimpse of regret,
She smiles away those numerous
Scars on her beautiful skin.

O what a great and true love!
My mother! My mother!
What shall I use to pay
This price?
From Nigeria, a student.

VALOR NOT BY WAR

Men of valor don't resort to guns.
Only the weak make war their resort.
This dark fog called war
Should not penetrate into this soil.
The matching foot of mighty men
Toward the battlefield are shaking
The earth, and their intense reluctance
To halt this match
Is causing a great earthquake.

Those who are instigating
And beating this drum of war
Are only after their own selfish aims.
Their heads are filled with plans to attain
Their national interest.
With deceit, they compel us to war,
Causing hatred among humankind
For more money with which to purchase their ammunition.

Brave men resort to words,
Not to the sword, not to guns, not to blood.
It is obsolete to buy arms to make women
Widows and to make children fatherless.
It's of no use to make a peaceful land

A gory land to show supremacy over others,
Whether of the same race or not.

Ask them, those who are warriors,
Ask them the song they sang in the desert,
If in each of their verses they remembered family.
In each chorus they sing of their wish to return home safely
And how bitter the sting of death will feel.
They envisage how lovely it will be
When love has hypnotized every heart.
They wish there was nothing like war
With blood and tears. They sing those songs.
Don't we think about the women and the children?

Warriors are said to be those who return home alive.
What about those gallant men
Who lost their lives in war?
Those who fought to their last breath
With aching foot but remained gallant,
Who fought days' unrest with hunger,
Those who drank their urine to survive?
But at the end their wives and children
Were not remembered and abandoned.

We only see the beginning of this war.
No one knows where it will end.

Abdulazeez Ishaq was born in the late 1980s to a family of six as the last child. He attended primary and secondary school in Osun State, Nigeria. He studied chemistry at Federal University of Technology, Akure. He enjoys reading and writing for pleasure. He is married with children.

THE OIL LAMP

Prior to the advent of electricity,
Preceding petroleum,
Before the advent of the solar lamp,
There existed the oil lamp
Lighting up streets and homes.

Illuminating its glow at night,
Glowing so brightly and beautifully in the dark,
Radiating so brilliantly from afar,
Reaching very far
But not too close,

The oil lamp keeps it base in darkness,
Lights up its environment
Just as my African siblings are
Quick to fault others
But see not their own faults.

My brothers see the glow in others,
Are impressed by the success of others,
Criticizes others' adversities,
Waste time analyzing others,
And never access themselves.

They speak woe upon others for plowing their path,
For wearing Italian shoes and
Peruvian and Brazilian hairstyles,
Choosing chemical in cans,
Admiring french fries and pizza,

Neglecting African-made products.
They have no regard for our delicacies,
Our fresh foods and vegetables.
Our batik tie-dyes are obsolete.
Indeed, a mere oil lamp

Couldn't help my brothers see gold beneath their noses.
They leave treasure in pursuit of pleasure,
Running from pillar to post
In search of what others possess,
Indeed, just as an oil lamp.

Could we retrace our steps?
Could we try mending our ways?
Shifting the lamp
To reveal the bounties it envelops.
Africans. The oil lamp.

RICHES AFTER RUINS

After night cometh, morning.
After sunset, the moon arrives.
After life comes death.
After summer lies spring.

Nothing begins
Without an end.
No race ever starts
Without a finish line.

At the end of pain
Lies thy gain.
At the end of this darkness
Lies thy light.

The dried grass thou see around
Germinates when rain comes.
The trees that wither now
Sprout when it's spring.

Adults who walk about
Once crawled.
They can run now,
But they've being staggering for a long time.

The struggle seems endless,
But success is around the corner.
The hunt is hurting.
Thy riches are right here.

Africa will bloom in blossom.
Grooming may drain blood to a pint,
But standing in our fragmented whole,
Thy defiance will define thy glory.

Naphtali Festus Adda is from Nigeria State, Tara LGA, Wukari.

DEAR PLATEAU

What tragedy is this?
Why is our peace into broken pieces?
Have we committed a sin?
Dear plateau,
What image are we portraying?
What will tourists see when they flock to town?
Which sound will their cameras make when the shutter is tripped?
Will it be the same *click* sound of our cries?
When has blood turned to water?
Or do they find pasture on our head?
Why do they succumb to blood as if they have a thirst to quench?
Are they "herdsmen" or "head men"?
Oh! Why won't I cry?
When there are trails of debt and cries of woe,
When a herd is worth more than a head,
When our cries are melodious rhythm in our leaders' ears.
Ah! Tell me why I shouldn't cry.

Dan Okafor is the fiery, Nigerian born writer and awareness coach, of the Igbo ethnic nationality. He was born in Delta State of Nigeria on the 27th day of September, 1970.

Having acquired both his primary and secondary education in his home town he went on to acquire professional training as a teacher, and in 1993 graduated in flying colors in the department of Mathematics/Economics from the prestigious College of Education, Agbor.

His very simple educational background not withstanding, Dan is multi talented as an accomplished classroom teacher, artist, creativity coach and motivational writer. Lately he joined the league of aspiring poets and bloggers.

He has a passion for excellence and would stop at nothing to see that things are done the right way, even if it means inconveniencing himself and walking alone.

AFRICA, SAVE ME!

I am not going to sing any song of Africa's vulgar heroism,
Nor strain my ink to write an ode to some proud warriors in ancestral savanna.
I am not here to mock the bardic landscape
With bellowing trumpet sounds from the mighty elephant tusks poached without conscience,
Nor pretend that all is well as I watch the lion king,
With ruthless mercilessness, bite its next victim—an easy meal—to extinction.

I will not shrug it off
As the hyenas and the crocs
Engage and fight each other to the death
Over a piece of meatless bone,
The carcasses of fallen African heroes dancing naked in the sun.
I will bother no more with the confused entreaties of souls languishing in the pit of hell,
Souls who make a sport out of prayer.
For, like they are, they believe their god must be deaf and dumb.
And instead of looking inward, they believe they must pray harder.

Hell: it is in Nigeria—suffering and smiling.
Hell: it is in Libya—human parts for money.
Hell: it is somewhere in Syria.

Hell: it is in sub-Saharan Africa
With its litany of economic woes.
Hell: it is in every soul looking on,
Watching, doing nothing as innocent blood daily is spilled on the altar of
Bloated egos looking down on a frustrated race unable to give account of its stewardship.

I will cringe in horror
And succumb to the vituperations of my nausea-laden stomach.
I will throw out the dark sputum from my throat
And, with a sigh of indignation, summon the weak princes of Africa.

I will say to them:
Where have you been
As Africa has suffered
One tale of woe after another?
You pretend to be blind, deaf, and dumb,
Yet you subjugate your women to inferior order
And marry as many just for the fun of the count.
You pretend to be blind, deaf, dumb, and psychologically handicapped,
Yet you set up monuments in worship of your ego,
Instead of the worship of the Light.
Woe unto you! Hypocrites!
Shameless shadows of real being!
Caricatures of humanity!
No one is coming to save you but yourself.
You are the ones you are waiting for.
You are your dreams come true.
Nothing in particular is primordially wrong with you;
You manufacture your problems by yourself.
You allow greed and impunity to get the better part of your humanity,
Until you became the exact symbol of everything dark.

O Africa,
Overflowing with scum and vermin as you are,
You await another Moses?
What will he come to do this time?
How will you treat him? Will you heed his word?
Will you obey him?
Or in defiance will you dance around another golden calf of transience
Erected by your ever-burgeoning vanity
And ask who made him a prince and a judge?

Africa,
Stop asking what to do!
You know what to do!
Stop shortchanging yourself.
Stop selling your children into slavery.
Stop conniving with the greedy merchants
From the north, south, east, and west.
Stop selling off your lands and people while remaining perpetually needy.
Martin Luther King already admonished you.
Mandela also echoed it:
Education is the light of the soul and the key to prosperity!
Empower your children.
Give them the right education.
Stop teaching them how to steal from the common good,
How to hold on to power endless.
Replace the dark polluted waters of their hearts
With the pure fount of truth and wisdom.
Unite!
Establish and sustain strong institutions of governance.
Away with mediocrity.
Let your very best of the best take charge in everything.
Uphold justice, purity, and love.
Live by a code. Practice what you preach.

Banish gender inequality.
Above all,
Know that it is possible to be free.
Know that the dream is its own fulfillment,
That you are enough to achieve whatever it is you want to achieve.

Then,
The wells of self-pity will dry up,
The pyramids will rise again,
The end linking up with the beginning.
Africa will arise afresh to lead humanity,
And the world will know peace.

THE EFFIGY OF SELF-RIGHTEOUSNESS

Sin:
A hapless,
Homeless,
Mindless vagabond
Begotten by African parents,
Hatched into a thousand mutations in American, European, and Asian laboratories,
And doctored by unseen masters of the yoke.

I remember vividly
Just as if it was yesterday
The eleven-year monstrous onslaught
When from 1991 to 2002, all hell broke loose in Sierra Leone,
Foday Sankoh chanting, "Operation No Living Thing!"
With Sam Bockarie, the "Mosquito," an officer commanding the RUF,
And justice, with the begging bowl, failing to bring home even a damned coin!

Yes, I remember,
Just as if it was yesterday,
The hundred days of sheer madness,
When in April of 1994,

Ethnic Hutus went on rampage,
Slaughtering more than a million Tutsis,
Their brothers and sisters of a common ancestry.
One hundred dark days of utter nightmare.
The world went blind, deaf, and dumb.
They did nothing to stop the carnage.
Why? Maybe because it happened on African soil.

Imagine
The slaughters!
The maimings!
The amputations!
The gang rapes!
The sex slavery!
The betrayals!
The evil alliances!
The human trafficking!
The impunity of Akin the rat drummer boy dancing the *surugede* in the palace of the king.

Now, fast-forward:
Libya,
Syria,
Nigeria!
Corpses winning medals in skimmington rides,
Inhumane humanity blind, deaf, and dumb,
One Iliad of hopelessness after another
One thing linking them all up: the urge for control.
The African's propensity to linger in sweet intoxication,
The love of power reducing ordinary men to nothing but confused deities
Like Lot's wife of the infamous Sodom and Gomorrah.

Reality check:

Look closely, anywhere in the world
Where war is the national language,
Where daily
Breakfast is served by bleeding mothers
And where the parched souls of future generations damned
Fry on the grills and pyres of the most demeaning forms of existence.
The people never rise above mere animal existence.

Is it the outward forms of the atrocities committed we should gaze upon,
Or the underlying philosophy behind these wars we must revisit?
Does the thinking that some war is justifiable really make them justified?
What about the thinking that some people deserve to die
While some live on as if sinless, with machetes and guns and bows and arrows brandished as toothpicks
After many luxurious meals of fire and brimstone
With which they send unrepentant souls to Hades?

Let us change the paradigms.
Let it be said of going to war
That we choose war knowing that war is wrong!
Let it be written that we know we have other options better than war!
That we choose war over peace since it is easier to kill than to save!
We choose war as our best friends, because they reinforce the lies we want to hear.
We choose war for no other reason than self-centeredness.
Superiority is a complex mold of sandcastles,
The propensity to shine, to let one's ego flare up in lurid self-praise.
War—the damned effigy of self-righteousness
Sculpted by the ever relentless intellect!

Let's stop these needless wars.
Let's outlaw all these hopeless operations:
Operation Crocodile Smile, killing with smiling fangs, to decimate and silence the voice of the weak;

Operation Python Dance—the first time pythons without feet have been seen to dance anywhere in the world.
We humans must realize
We do not own this earth,
Africans and their conniving masters in particular.
We are guests here; we should be agreeable guests.
To be agreeable is to obey the rules of our host's household.
To be agreeable is not to cause harm or havoc.
To be agreeable is not to overstay our welcome.
Let us be so agreeable that rules and billboards of do's and don'ts are no longer necessary.
Let us remember to fear only one thing: the inviolable sublimity of the Will divine—
To remember to sow only as we would like to reap
In order that our ledger account be balanced,
And a righteous handshake with righteousness
Be our just reward.

Reflections:
There is calm now.
We are now enjoying peace and harmony.
But, suddenly,
Robots
Without a mind of their own
Come marching toward us again,
Wielding weapons of war!
What do they want? They want war!
Always they seek justification for war!
They like to chant: "All is fair in war!"
But I say to them: "Nothing is fair in war!"
Not even the stinking good deeds
Of an overcelebrated United Nations.
Disunited United Nations
With its gifts of a thousand Trojan horses

And many Achilleses lying in wait,
Waiting to reap a thousand years of glory,
Making another's misfortune their fortune.
Many will not remember how to love again,
For they have gazed too deep into the abyss,
So deep that the abyss gazed back at them.
In taming the monster, they themselves have become monsters.
To keep the peace requires the courage to uphold justice, purity, and love.

THE ORACLE OF SILENCE

Who among men born of a women
Could swallow the unfortunate pill of knowing he is an African
And still remain unperturbed?
Countless times have I regurgitated this bitter pill.
Countless times have I slept and awakened since contemplating my destiny,
Hoping to find myself in a kind and homely new world.

But lo!
The nightmares are even more real!
I sought for one to castrate my memories
And blot out every remembrance of
This accursed heritage,
But that too didn't work.
A more formidable odyssey, endless,
Is continually being spun right before me
By some hands unseen, it seems, shrouded in profound secrecy and mystery
And mortal placidity.
Even Ulysses sufferings at the hand of
The imperial Poseidon
Is child's play compared to what humans in Africa are going through.

At once I concluded I must intercede

As an African for Africa, as Africa in person.
I must wager with the forces of life and death.
I must gird my loins once and for all, and confront this monstrous oracle called silence,
And ask, "What is my crime? Why is
Being an African a choice between two evils?
Where in the journey of being human did I get it wrong?
Speak! Speak to me! Prove yourself a man and speak to me!
Prove to me you didn't connive with the sower
To sow me as a thorn, and my siblings as oaks and unicorns!"
Then, I heard a deep rumbling voice,
A quaking thunder from the bowels of the world:

"Despondent one," it thundered,
"*I am!*
Neither fairy nor monster!
I created neither Negro nor Caucasian nor Mongolian.
I scattered the seed of the human spirit
Fairly enough and with the same measure of goodness and purpose.
You yourself, by yourself alone, gave yourself the name Africa!
I care not what you call yourself
Or what you allow yourself to be called.
I care only how you define what you are called by your deeds.
Have you forgotten how you wrestled me to a standstill in the presence of your brothers, asking for the blessing of wisdom?
Have you forgotten how I warned you that you asked a little too early?
That wisdom, swallowed too early in the day, could prove dangerous, even fatal?"

Yet, you insisted,
Wherefore I anointed you before the high noon of the day.
And you became dazed and bewitched
By powers you could not control.
You suffered in the ensuing confusion

Until, seeing your desperation, I gave you the help of a healing flower.
You took it without further ado, drank from its petals, and healed.
Meanwhile, many of your children were already beaten beyond recognition.
They died.
The best among your brothers, having studied the situation, decided to leave the toxic environment,
While the average and less than average lingered behind in Circe's bed.
Now I ask you, Africa: where is my crime in all of this?

If you want to truly heal and regain your humanity,
You must descend from your precarious perch,
Descend from your exalted altars of "I know nothing" and "I know everything." Life is more than knowing and not knowing.
Life is being, and
To be is to remain natural, simple, and open to change, for
Life is the only constant there is, and
Change is the only permanent reality. Return to the infancy of adulthood now, and rebuild from there.
Otherwise, Scylla you may have outwitted. But Charybdis you are still within reach of.

Put on the whole armor of humility.
Have the humanity and courage
To do the needful now, while you still can.
Regain all that you have lost, now, while you can still bargain with life.
I am not asking you to be yourself anymore, for that has not helped.
I am asking you to be who and what you are meant to be.

VIRTUES OF THE QUEEN

Standing
At the
Summit
Of Kilimanjaro,
I see wildebeests
Buffalos,
Zebras,
Impalas,
Giraffes,
Elephants,
Hyenas,
Wild dogs.
I see them run helter-skelter,
The lion queen forever on their trails,
The Serengeti and the Mara
Trembling with wild expectations.

Africa,
My relentless home!
You give life to the strong and
Take it from the weak.
I surveyed the entire African
Landscape,
Thanks to my useless curiosity,

And I found
That the strongest and the fastest
Prey on the weakest and the slowest.
The corollary among *Homo sapiens* is more horrible than we dare to contemplate:
Other species kill mainly for food or territorial integrity.
Humankind alone kill to gratify its ego.

I saw that the strong get stronger
While the weak upgrade toward becoming strong.
No one is getting weaker,
For in Africa
There is no place for what is weak.
The toughest of the jungle
Pitch tents with the invisible giants who roam the vast mountain scape.
Even the mountains themselves seem to
Have a soft spot for ruggedness.
The whole world stands awed and bemused by the African spectacle,
Life in its raw jungle ferocity,
And it is good: only humankind is sham, in all its ways.

An honest attempt
To reduce Africa's ills,
To save it from
Poverty and shame
And effect true healing,
Mmust begin
With a total and violent shift in
Consciousness.
Mindfulness, not a blind chance!
Let the African queen arise
And take a dose of inspiration from the lioness queen.
With tireless zeal
She hunts, heals, feeds, and keeps her

Family united.

Virtue lives with the queen!
She knows her place, and she fills it.
She takes what is hers with agility and swiftness of mind.
With a fearsome menace does she tear down any who dares her might!
Nearly independent, she never nags her king.
She never asks why she must humble herself before him
And allow the king take the lion's share of the fruits of her escapades.
She knows her weakness—her undying loyalty to the king—
A weakness that protects and saves her in times of trouble.
For a queen is nothing without her king.
Nor ever does the king take her for granted.
They both know they cannot survive alone; they need each other.

The African woman must arise,
Arise, and attack the injustice, mediocrity, and lawlessness in Africa.
Arise with a terrible relentlessness
With the king's and prince's and princess' swords
Gleaming in a cacophony of a thousand focused thrusts.
For man shall go to war with metal blades and swords and bows and arrows,
But woman shall go to war with the blazing and consuming fire of the iron will
Rooted in the laws of God, for the good of humanity.
Evil is winning in Africa because the African woman is silently complicit.

APPENDIX

BOOK REVIEW OF SAVE AFRICA

"Save Africa" a modern poetry and short story anthology, edited by, David Gretch, is now on the market. It's an exceptional book with the most creative writings I have behold. It surpasses many books of poetry and short stories, I have reviewed. It's inspiring, uplifting, and motivating. It generates wonderful thoughts of Africa, thus, stimulating the mind, body and soul. Readers of poetry and literature, should read this book to acquire wisdom and understanding. These great poets and authors are generators of modern literary and poetic thoughts. Their collective inspiration based on creative visionary style is awesome.

This anthology consists of male and female scholars. They poured their hearts out with ink of diamond and gold in penning words of great revelations, mysteries, and wonders. Their articulation is for everyone to read and enjoy for upliftment with a smiling face of gratitude. Their majestical collaboration of unity are from, South Africa, Uganda, Nigeria, and Kenya.

Nzogi Olivia Osuoha, from Nigeria, begins the introduction of this great anthology (pages: xiii-xviii), with the poem, "Natural Gift." Selected words from the poem are as follows:

> *Rocky valley with green leaves. Rushing water of real nature*
> *As white as snow. So rich to flow.*
> *Rocky land of God. Flowing with milk and honey*
> *So lovely to behold. So dear to be grateful for.*

These are magnificent words about God's creation. They indicate beauty and excellence of Africa's richness with elegance for others to come and experience.

Nancy Ndeke, from Kenya, is next with an essay. Her narration is entitled, "Who un-Africanized Us?" The following are selected lines from her piece addressing Africa's generosity and warmth as follows:

Noted for its generosity of spirit and warmth of its people, it is a land that is indeed beautiful to behold. However, this beauty, generosity, and warmth has been visited with horrid repercussions time and again with the passage of time since the first visitors landed on Africa's shores. Hunting for spices, slaves, elephant tusks, and the pure bliss of exotic sightings of a race of black men.

She continues by setting the stage of how such a beautiful land with generous people experienced horrid repercussions from visitors. Each seeking their own glory without any consideration for life and health of the people as follows:

The consequence is evident in the struggles for identity and in the bitterness of those uprooted from their motherlands, given new names and tongues up to this day.

Through association with the visitor, through his assumed superiority as one educated, our man, when the government of the visitor came to claim territory, had no choice but to join ranks with his mentor. He was effectively de-Africanized.

De-Africanization is a false concept leveraged to downplay the hand of the actual criminals, corporeal entities who would do anything and everything for profit, including committing murder. The African is a small player satisfied with less, while much is sent home abroad for the real war instigators.

She ends her narration by showing through analogy, that the true de-Africanization came from the people of Africa as small players. They assisted the invaders in looting Africa of its wealth, resources, riches, and its people.

Poetry and Stories from South Africa

Morgana VientoLameculos, from South Africa, beings the next section of the anthology (pages: I-5). It begins with a Commentary as follows:

> *I have watched my country go from a safe place to a place of mayhem, crime, and political turmoil. And I have seen its transition from apartheid to a free democracy. With the latter came a free-for-all attitude—a system of riots and plunder, of racism and hate, of oppression and rape. Our people live in fear and in poverty amid unemployment and crime-ridden communities. "It is time for the world to see, to know ... It is time for change!"*

She elaborates her disappointments because of crime, poverty, and unemployment, and highlights governance by criminals. This has resulted in the people being burdened by undermining leadership, affecting their peace, growth, and prosperity.

In the poem, "Cried My Beloved Country." He shows hope for South Africa and its people as follows:

> *Cry, my beloved Africa! Write with your tears a brand-new song— A song of hope, a song of peace. Shout it out with voices strong, For tears will dry and hope prevail. Where love is abundant, Hope and peace will never fail!*

Poems and Stories from Uganda

Kabedoopong Piddo Ddibe'st, is first poet from Uganda (pages: 9-103). He teaches English, literature, and is a literary writer. His first poem entitled, "Served the poet more papers," in very interesting. Excerpts are as follows:

> *Serve the poet more papers. Serve him the cracking clips Greater miracles are performed by the barrel of the pen than the guns have ever done. Serve him not the people's meat but the barrel of the pen; And what is more— the sick world is healed.*

He laminates seeking justice for the people. Such and awesome trait of wisdom. He wants to see the poet's pen instead of bullets from the barrel of a gun.

In his next poem entitled, "Ruping and Adyadwee," he acts as Ruping seeking the love of Anyadwee. Her parents are against their relationship for a variety of reasons. The following are selected lines from the piece:

> *(Ruping): You're my beautiful black beauty; your skin is the skin of shea nut oil, Glistening like a dust of goldfish… (Adyadwee): My beloved man, look into my starry eyes. I have something to tell you: You are the joy of my life. I will fall dead before them… (Ruping): O daughter of the lily, the valley of the red roses, love me the way I am… (Adyadwee): I will marry you, my dove. The clouds are pregnant with golden rains. (Ruping): I will kiss your dimpled cheeks. And make love bloom in the wild, Where no forbidden fruits grow white… (Adyadwee): I love your love song, darling; you're killing me here softly. Hold my hands and take me away. Take me forever, now and today.*

This story continues in a series of poems regarding both individuals, with wonderful words between Ruping and Adyadwee.

Obella Stephen, from Uganda is the next poet (pages: 104-120). He is a literature teacher, lyricist, and stage performer. He is the founder of Writers Foundation. His poem entitled, "Raise No Weapons," with selected lines are as follows:

> *Raise no more weapons, nor glittering swords, for the poet's pen wilt rust 'em by liquid words. Fold no fists; knock no man down, for he who started war digs a grave of his own. Divine's thy ink that preaches peace so fair. Love, unite from toenail to thine last hair. Let no big-bellied politician rape the book of law. Let world peace, as candles, burn on and on, for we desire a world with o'er whelming hate gone.*

He justifiable pleas for his countrymen to live peacefully and avoid conflict. He sees the divine ink of the pen as a resolution by writing instead of fighting.

Edakasi Daniel, is the next poet from Uganda. He is a teacher of English language and literature. Selected lines from his poem, "Grain of Peace," are as follows:

> *A peaceful mind grind rocks of no end. It starts with your grandfather, and goes to all your ancestral grandchildren. A peaceful mind unlocks all the doors of the Chinese temple. Your culture needs your peace. You need peace in you, because it starts with you. And all your neighbors, friends, and relatives. You will build generations under your thin legs. And generations will be your peace.*

He pleas for peace among his people, and sees a peaceful mind as an asset. The initiation of peace starts with an individual and passes on to future generations.

Poems and Stories from Kenya

Nancy Ndeke, is the first poet from Kenya (pages 133—185). She is a poet and author. She has two poetry e-books available on Amazon.

com. Her poem is entitled, "Africa." Selected lines from her poem are as follows:

> *Return to your senses. The answer you seek is in your heart. Moderate your acquisition. Touch another with kindness.*
> *Rewrite your story for tomorrow with better adjectives. This perpetual song of woe is tiresome. Africa! It is possible to be right and just, to be guided by the human conscience.*

She pleas for Kenya to return to its senses, and project a new and wonderful picture of Africa. She wants a change in its mission and vision, however, not the type that shows death camps and destruction of villages. She needs to see a new Africa.

Benjamin Chelangat, is the next poet. He is a graduate of English literature from Kyambogo University. His poem "Buried without Graves," was inspired from his urge to unravel the consequences of wars around the world. Selected lines are as follows:

> *On the mountaintop, fire spoke the language of no return: of thunder and boom! They were buried without graves, without the teary vigil that would console the bereaved ... in the land where bullets pass the sentence from the arena of mortality. By the wild, joyous scavengers who performed the funerals in the jungles without the church hymn. Now, they rest without graves in the land that is never their home.*

Philip Mainge, is the next poet from Kenya (pages 189-203), followed by Dr. Joan Ngunnzi. Selected lines from her poem, "The Last Bullet," are as follows:

> *He fired. She fired. He missed. She missed. He fired again and missed but followed with a club. So, she realized it was war. No longer a funny game. Peekaboo. She would make proper use of her last bullet!*

She speaks of an ongoing controversy between two individuals reflecting hate and discontentment. The poet's plea is for this type of activity to be erased from Africa.

Poetry from Nigeria

Ngozi Olivia Osuoha, is the first poet from Nigeria (208-230). Her writing, "The Transformation Train and Letter to My Unborn," is published in Kenya and Canada. It's available on Amazon. Selected lines from her poem, "Political Monsters," are as follows:

> *They are the gangsters in many disciplines. They are the tricksters misguiding the populace. They are the masters playing every card. They are the chameleon in beautiful colors. Political monsters, the Cankerworms that stir the storm, and trouble our form. The termite that eats our norm and destroys our reform. Political monsters, the beasts after our peace.*

She lays out with great descriptive excellence resonating in vivid images, the leaders of her country. She wants a change in leadership and conditions for the better welfare of the people.

Etim Bassey Onyam, is the next poet from Nigeria (232-235). He has many Golden Awards in poetry. He is the founder of Home of African Poetry and Splendid Stories, which inspires many poets. Selected lines from his poem, "The Untrodden Paths of Africa," are as follows:

> *Who shall lead the adventure to these paths? The paths to which the nationalists only opened the ways, hoping this posterity would do the undone ...Arise, O ye budding compatriots of Africa, for these paths must be explored to salvage this sinking continent!*

He describes many paths he has seen. Some entrapping Mother Africa in a hideous quagmire and perdition, others with corruption and looting.

Paths at whose entryways lie dry bones. He expresses his disgusts of the governors and leaders failing the people.

Nseobong Edem, is the next poet from Nigeria (236-255). He's an award-winning poet and has won many international-based awards. Lines from his poem, "Farewell Song," are as follows:

> *'Tis not an ode. But it's just a grief-stricken song that craves no rapping of the gong. No bridge shall beckon for us to cross over our integrity, Nor shall our temple lose its innocence. Who among us will not feel a happy rage and sensuous muttered joy, to watch an ailing sister's weeping lips? If ever you deserve fair treatment, the same as the elite class, please echo this farewell song. And let it in. It brings freedom! For this farewell song is one of freedom to save Africa.*

He uses a series of questioning techniques to draw the reader into the poem for a deeper understanding. He relates situations not right for the people and desires a new day.

Chidi Nwosu, is the next poet from Nigeria (256-260). He is an entrepreneur, poet, writer, social and political commentator. Selected lines form his poem, "One Day," are as follows:

> *One day after the vultures picked clean the cadavers and the only memories Left are seas of white bones, we shall remember the peace we should've sown decades ago. One day after the famine precipitated by wars and lawlessness, we shall remember the rule of law we had forsaken. One day after the country is balkanized, each will be left holding a fragile piece, a peace worthless.*

He engages in direct speech and thoughts about what should have taken place in Africa. His lamentation is about actions the leaders and politicians failed to take while in power to prevent atrocities. His vision leads him to believe greater is yet to come.

Francis Annagu, is the next poet from Nigeria (261-267). He lives in Southern Kaduna, and is referred to as Southern Kaduna's most prominent poetic voice. Selected lines from his poem, "Our Land in a Desert Trough," are as follows:

> *Our land potted in the scorched trough of a little desert pond, cracked in the ravaging sun; a treasury of coins and contracts. Our famished land drank a lot of wine from the vulture's pot of greed, ever since the masses trooped the parliament gates. The poor are hungry since their corn farms have no drizzle to grow grains in the harmattan. Pounding boots announce the rancor in the overblowing grime of turbulence and the heat that harbors our cricks, but our leaders are merry behind electric gates, turning away their transient smiles from the tumults of our land.*

Such a devastating poem. He cries his heart out for justice regarding those who have nothing, against those who have. He believes the vulture's pot of greed has become a part of Africa.

Udekwe Chikadibia, is the next poet from Nigeria (268-270). He is currently studying English language and literature. Selected lines from his poems, "I Was Made to Believe," are as follows:

> *I was made to believe that our leaders are werewolves, that I have to believe strongly that they're our woes. I was made to believe this right from my infancy. I was made to believe that the lazy youths are the leaders of blind tomorrow, but the youths I am seeing now are in sweet sorrow. But dear listener, be informed that we practice gerontocracy, and our leaders are not wane werewolves, and the lazy youths are the leaders of blind tomorrow.*

His words are striking as to what he was made to believe. Here he illustrates that his mind was ill advised, and seeks not be a part of that belief system anymore. He has a new and different outlook on life based on his experience.

Nosar Philips, is the next poet from Nigeria (271-274). He is a business-minded person who craves joy in writing. Specific lines from his poem, "Untitled (Amope)" are as follows:

> *The scariest disguise I could wear. The picture of a beast that children saw at Erie Junction. On the surface I am happy. But I had something pursuing me. I am quite the Masquerade Man. Everybody here thinks I'm perfect. They can't look inside. Barren women see us as Priapus. And at Ekpenede I saw Amope. Following her was imperative. Amope, all the way from Ile Nfe, I must follow you.*

He is grief stricken, and is ashamed of his situation of masquerading which is a state of affair. This requires him to wear a mask to disguised his true and inner self. He seeks an escape.

David Chukwudi Njoku, is the next poet from Nigeria (2750-282). He is a faith preacher and a lover of poetry. His utmost desire is to make a positive impact on the world with God's Word and poetry. Excerpts from his poem, "Save Africa: The Preacher Bleeds," are as follows:

> *Hey, you there, I'm here. With the words of the Creator. To bring you salvation from the scripture. My preaching is against, the rulers of injustice, the killers of destinies, the parasitic flu, the jungle justice. Arise and pick up. Pick up your pen against these poisonous asps. Their viper's tongues shall we slay, slaying it by picking up our pens to swallow their darkness with light from our pen.*

He calls on everyone for support to fight corruption, and for unity to fight against, nepotism, racism, tribalism, and emerging wars. He considers such as disheartening, damaging, and cancerous. He calls for unity and uprising to correct the problem.

Nwankwo Christian, the next poet from Nigeria (283-284). His interest in poetry grew in high school as he reads many poetry books and articles. Excerpts from his anaphora styled poem entitled, "I Am a Black, and African American," are as follows:

> *I am the voice crying for your help. I am the one stolen from my father's land. I am the color you look upon like something thrown away. I am the one whose children you killed. I am the slave whose sweat and blood built your nation. I am the one they gave freedom to but still imprisoned. I am a black, an African American.*

Here is a new twist in the anthological poems. He writes in the anaphora form and style with direct language. The poet is not only from Africa he is also an African American. He states historical facts with concrete language of his experience on both continents.

Ayomide Samuel, is the next poet from Nigeria (285-289). Excerpts from his poem, "Magnificent Image," are as follows:

> *Heroes on the battlefield of motherhood, a superb image of God's dexterity. With tears, blood, a yell, and a smile, she fights her battle to see her seed yielding sweet fruit. Her precious gold and pride she sows to build her nation strong and mighty. She smiles away those numerous scars on her beautiful skin. O what a great and true love! My mother! What shall I use to pay this price?*

He is proud of the heroes from his motherland, and is pleased of the battles they fought to yield sweet fruit. He is dismayed about the price one has to pay regarding the cost.

Abdulazeez Ishaq, is the next poet from Nigeria (290-294). He studied chemistry at Federal University of Technology, Akure. Excerpts from his poem, "The Oil Lamp," are as follows:

> *Prior to the advent of electricity, preceding petroleum, before the advent of the solar lamp, there existed the oil lamp, lighting up streets and homes. The oil lamp keeps it base in darkness, lights up its environment. My brothers see the glow in others. Are impressed by the success of others. Criticizes others' adversities. Waste time analyzing others, and never access themselves. Could we retrace our steps? Could we try mending our ways? Shifting the lamp to reveal the bounties it envelops. Africans. The oil lamp.*

He is proud of the oil lamp and how it has provided for them. He shows discontent with his siblings desiring foreign products instead of from Africa, and would like to see a change.

Naphtali Festus Adda, is the final poet from Nigeria (295-296). Excerpt from his poem entitled, "Dear Plateau, "are as follows:

> *What tragedy is this? Why is our peace into broken pieces? Have we committed a sin? What will tourists see when they flock to town? Why do they succumb to blood as if they have a thirst to quench? Are they "herdsmen" or "head men"? Why do they succumb to blood as if they have a thirst to quench? Ah! Tell me why I shouldn't cry.*

He is overwhelmed by the current situation showing lack of peace in his country. He questions many situations and wonders how they will affect the tourists visiting his town. He is not satisfied with the shedding of blood.

Conclusion

It was sincerely a pleasure for me reviewing this anthology. The poets and authors are awesome. They are great people striving for excellence in their craft while using the muse eloquently. They are ingenious with their inspiration of the written word to uplift others.

The forms of poems and writings in this anthology include many styles and skills. I have read poems covering the narrative free form style. I have enjoyed eloquently written poems using a variety of descriptive excellence resonating with many vivid images. Poems with techniques, such as, concrete language, figurative and imaginative words, and anaphora style are just great.

The inspiring tone of each poem moves the words easily down the page. The questioning technique draws the reader into the poem for a greater understanding of the author's vision. One is able to feel the smiles form the authors' faces while reading, based on the inspiration resonating from the poems. Their use of analogy is uplifting, and use of imagery is wonderful. Their use of similes and metaphors make the poems more imaginative and creative.

Furthermore, the narrations in this anthology are outstanding. Their use of symbology portraying various things are impacting. Verbs showing actions in the narrations are elevating. Their use of proper tense moves the narrations in the right directions without confusion.

Finally, the theme and tone of "Save Africa," certainly resonate through the anthology with reverence. They reflect in each poem and essay with precision. They generate images that are glorious, and devasting on the opposite end, with creativity and imagination. They leave the mind seeking more to be fulfilled with dynamic words and thoughts from these great authors.

This is an awesome anthology to read. One must get to know these poets and writers, and keep a visual for their next publication, to continue experiencing such creative thoughts and poetry.

They may be contacted through their publisher at: (publisher's email).

The reviewer of this anthology, Joseph S. Spence, Sr., is the author of three poetry books. He is published in many forums and have received numerous awards including: Poetry Ambassador's Medal (USA), Independent Poet Laureate (USA), and Poetry Bard (UK). He is a retired military officer who resides in Wisconsin. He may be reached at: jspence078@gmail.com.

www.ingramcontent.com/pod-product-compliance
Lightning Source LLC
Chambersburg PA
CBHW021422070526
44577CB00001B/20